Jimi Hendrix

MUSICIAN

Black Americans of Achievement

LEGACY EDITION

Muhammad Ali

Maya Angelou

Josephine Baker

Johnnie Cochran

Frederick Douglass

W.E.B. Du Bois

Marcus Garvey

Savion Glover

Alex Haley

Jimi Hendrix

Langston Hughes

Jesse Jackson

Scott Joplin

Coretta Scott King

Martin Luther King, Jr.

Malcolm X

Bob Marley

Thurgood Marshall

Jesse Owens

Rosa Parks

Colin Powell

Chris Rock

Sojourner Truth

Harriet Tubman

Nat Turner

Booker T. Washington

Oprah Winfrey

Jimi Hendrix

MUSICIAN

Dale Evva Gelfand

CHELSEA HOUSE
PUBLISHERS
An imprint of Infobase Publishing

Jimi Hendrix

Copyright © 2006 by Infobase Publishing

All rights reserved. No part of this book may be reproduced or utilized in any form or by any means, electronic or mechanical, including photocopying, recording, or by any information storage or retrieval systems, without permission in writing from the publisher. For information, contact:

Chelsea House
An imprint of Infobase Publishing
132 West 31st Street
New York NY 10001

Library of Congress Cataloging-in-Publication Data

Gelfand, Dale Evva, 1944-
  Jimi Hendrix / Dale Gelfand. — Legacy ed.
      p. cm. — (Black Americans of achievement)
  Includes bibliographical references (p.   ), discography (p.   ), and index.
  ISBN 0-7910-9214-3 (hardcover)
  1. Hendrix, Jimi—Juvenile literature. 2. African American rock musicians—United States—Biography—Juvenile literature. I. Title. II. Series.
  ML3930.H45G45 2006
  787.87'166092—dc22   2006004574

Chelsea House books are available at special discounts when purchased in bulk quantities for businesses, associations, institutions, or sales promotions. Please call our Special Sales Department in New York at (212) 967-8800 or (800) 322-8755.

You can find Chelsea House on the World Wide Web at
http://www.chelseahouse.com

Series and cover design by Keith Trego, Takeshi Takahashi

Printed in the United States of America

Bang FOF 10 9 8 7 6 5 4 3 2 1

This book is printed on acid-free paper.

All links and Web addresses were checked and verified to be correct at the time of publication. Because of the dynamic nature of the Web, some addresses and links may have changed since publication and may no longer be valid.

Contents

Birth of a Legend

Jimmy Hendrix the man was born on November 27, 1942. Jimi Hendrix the legend was born on June 18, 1967. That was the day that the Jimi Hendrix Experience played its first American gig. That was the day that Jimi Hendrix, who had returned to his native country from London, set the sold-out crowd of some 100,000 music fans afire with his guitar-playing pyrotechnics—then concluded his virtuoso performance by setting his Stratocaster guitar ablaze with lighter fluid. That was the day that Jimi Hendrix was catapulted onto the world stage. That was the day that Jimi Hendrix revolutionized rock music.

The setting was the Monterey International Pop Festival in Northern California, held at the Monterey County Fairgrounds. Tucked under a canopy of oak trees in the sunbelt of the Monterey Peninsula, the bucolic fairgrounds was not only the home of the annual county fair, it had also been the site of the renowned Monterey Jazz Festival since 1958. Now promoters wanted to try something new—a three-day outdoor festival that would be an incredible fusion of musical styles: rock and roll, jazz, R&B, blues, country blues, jazz, psychedelic rock, even Indian raga. The roster of 30-plus acts was a who's-who of 1960s pop music greats. Acts like Canned Heat, Booker T and the MGs, the Grateful Dead, Simon and Garfunkel, the Animals, the Butterfield Blues Band, Lou Rawls, the Jefferson Airplane, Otis Redding, Country Joe and the Fish, the Byrds, and the Mamas and the Papas were the primary drawing cards. Concertgoers, though, eagerly anticipated the performances of the lesser-known talent that had been getting plenty of buzz—especially the British band the Who; local Bay-area group Big Brother and the Holding Company, featuring singer Janis Joplin; and a rumored guitar master named Jimi Hendrix, who was said to have taken England by storm.

Intended as an event to legitimize and validate rock music for mainstream America, the Monterey International Pop Festival was the brainchild of John Philips, founder of the Mamas and the Papas. He realized that, to make the festival work, the musical artists would have to work for free—only their expenses would be paid. Astonishingly, with few exceptions, most of those asked agreed. The festival's board of directors was almost as stellar as the ultimate lineup—several Beatles, a couple of Rolling Stones, and the Beach Boys among them. It was Beatle Paul McCartney—an enthusiastic fan of Hendrix's who had been attending the guitarist's gigs since his arrival in London the September before—who had insisted that the Jimi Hendrix Experience be booked. A native of Seattle, Hendrix was far better known in England and throughout Europe—where he had been gaining an impressive reputation for his musicianship and his showmanship, especially with guitar icons like Brian Jones of the Rolling Stones, Jeff Beck of the Yardbirds, and Eric Clapton of Cream. Hendrix had not yet made such an impact in his own country. In fact, on a layover

Jimi Hendrix was virtually unknown in the United States before his appearance, shown here, at the Monterey International Pop Festival. His fiery performance at Monterey made him a legend.

in New York on his way to California, he was mistaken for a bellhop at his hotel. The Monterey International Pop Festival would instantly change all of that.

COUNTERCULTURE CULTURE

The festival was not just a place where like-minded rock fans could gather. It was also the first gathering of the counterculture, an event whose motto was "Music, Love, and Flowers." Indeed, John Philips wrote the hugely popular song "San Francisco (Be Sure to Wear Some Flowers in Your Hair)," made famous by singer Scott McKenzie, specifically for the festival. The celebrated "Summer of Love" occurred in 1967, when seemingly everyone under the age of 25 flocked to San Francisco's Haight-Ashbury district, and flower power was in full bloom. The United States was experiencing an extraordinary youth movement, a new sense of freedom that was reflected in the clothes and hairstyles of young people, in the art, and in the music. The cultural change was like a tidal wave that began in California and swept across the country with astonishing speed and power.

The Monterey festival proved to be a peaceful haven for these laid-back cultural revolutionaries, a place where people with shared beliefs could come together. The audience, as well as the musicians and their music, epitomized diversity. Monterey's proximity to San Francisco guaranteed a good turnout for the festival, and the Monterey city fathers had feared the worst: tens of thousands of runaways or drug-crazed hippies in the grip of wild debauchery. Though beads and fringe and peace symbols were the accessories of choice, and drugs (especially the recently popular LSD, tabs of which were given out like breath mints to the musicians backstage) were very much in evidence, the attendees were as polite and well-behaved as children on a school field trip. With so much benevolence, the police in their riot helmets ended up milling about with nothing to do but smile goofily—conceivably as a result of inadvertently inhaling the haze of marijuana smoke that floated over the field like low-lying fog—and enjoy the show themselves.

Making the festival possible required financial backing from record companies. "In return," Harry Shapiro and Caesar Glebbeek wrote in *Jimi Hendrix: Electric Gypsy*, "Monterey provided the companies with a supermarket of unsigned rock talent to give the monolithic corporations the youth credibility they now realized they needed." At the same time, the artists' managers realized that the festival might well be the ticket to fame that their clients desired. "Monterey [was] a festival of two worlds. Out front, many of the audience believed they were participating in an event that would help revolutionize society. Backstage, the executives were looking to revolutionize their [profits], while the managers lusted after big advances—which they got." One witness reported that the hottest action was not on the stage but at the makeshift bars, where the record industry bigwigs got into heated bidding wars.

The musicians, though, were primarily there to play for their fans and jam with one another. The festival got off to a rousing start on Friday evening with the Association singing its hit, "Along Comes Mary." Lou Rawls and Johnny Rivers followed, and then, representing the second wave of the British invasion, Eric Burdon and the Animals. Closing the Friday night show were Simon and Garfunkel doing their "59th Street Bridge Song (Feelin' Groovy)." Saturday afternoon showcased some of the best musicians of the San Francisco music scene, including Country Joe and the Fish, Quicksilver Messenger Service, the Steve Miller Band, and, in a passionate performance that blew everyone away and stole the show, Janis Joplin with Big Brother and the Holding Company. It was her first performance outside of San Francisco, and she would leap to international stardom. Saturday night's roster had the Jefferson Airplane flying high, the Byrds trying out their new country-rock sound, and soul singer Otis Redding. Redding drew such an ecstatic response from the largely white crowd that, as soon as he returned home to Georgia, he composed his smash hit "Sitting on the Dock of the Bay" as a tribute to the audience that had made him feel so welcome.

A SHOWDOWN BETWEEN GUITARISTS

Sunday's program was fairly loose. Ravi Shankar was set to be the sole artist that afternoon—the crowd initially grooved to his ragas, but after four hours of droning sitar, even the most avid fans of Indian music were sated and not many remained—and the Mamas and the Papas were to close the show that night. The rest of the acts, including the Grateful Dead, the Who, and the Jimi Hendrix Experience, were in a kind of line-up free-for-all. Jimi Hendrix and Pete Townshend, lead guitarist for the Who, knew each other well from the London music scene. Both were flamboyant, over-the-top performers who left their audiences gasping at their ability and their antics. Each usually finished up his set by smashing his guitar and trashing the stage. Figuring he would look like an idiot if he were to wreck his equipment after Hendrix had done the same thing, Townshend demanded that the Who play first. Hendrix was equally adamant that he should not have to follow the Who. Like two strutting roosters, the competitive musicians each insisted that the other should go on last. Things got pretty heated until Philips told them that the toss of a coin would decide the matter. Whoever won would go on first, and that would be that. Townshend won. Fueled by anger and LSD, Hendrix vowed, "I'm going to pull out all the stops."

Rising to the challenge, the Who played its set with a vengeance. As the band began its final song, Townshend told the audience, "This is where it all ends." The song climaxed with explosions and smoke; then Townshend smashed his guitar against the microphone stand over and over until it was nothing but kindling. The crowd went crazy. Egged on by the response, Keith Moon began flinging his drumsticks, and then mike stands and amps were thrown. Country Joe McDonald later noted, "It was kind of a combination of wrestling and music." By the end of the frenzy, equipment lay strewn all over the stage, and the Who—only popular before in their native England—had cemented their place in the rock-star firmament with talent and carnage. It was one heck of an act to have to follow.

As a sort of lull between two musical storms, the Grateful Dead played next, and Jerry Garcia mellowed the crowd with his soft melodies. Then Brian Jones of the Rolling Stones took the stage to announce the next act, introducing Hendrix as "a very good friend, a fellow countryman of yours," and "the most exciting performer I've ever heard."

Hendrix—stoked by adrenaline, pot, and acid—hit the stage carrying a Stratocaster guitar that he had hand-painted two days earlier. He was cloaked in psychedelic regalia: a gold-braided military jacket, a yellow ruffled shirt, red velvet pants, a feather boa, and hair in a wild, teased Afro. The band launched into "Killing Floor" by blues great Howlin' Wolf, followed immediately by "Foxey Lady," the bump-and-grind first cut on its debut album, *Are You Experienced*. Hendrix charged through his act with unrestrained joy and unabashed theatricality—his large hands holding his guitar in every imaginable position, toying with feedback, bending the banshee notes pouring from his amps. Eric Burdon (quoted in *Jimi Hendrix: The Ultimate Experience*) recalled, "This was the first time Jimi had the chance to play to his own people. So he just went for it.... He started out as a black American on Friday night.... By Sunday night he was an Apache warrior, just out to kill." Added musician David Crosby, "We all sat there with our jaws dropped. We couldn't believe anybody could do that. Nobody had ever seen or heard anybody play guitar like that before."

Then Hendrix addressed the audience. "Right now we'd like to do a little thing by Bob Dylan, a little thing called 'Like a Rolling Stone.'" This new guitar god invoking one of the heroes

Brian Jones of the Rolling Stones (right) and German model and singer Nico sit in the audience at the Monterey International Pop Festival. Jones introduced Hendrix at the festival, calling him "the most exciting performer I've ever heard."

of the cultural revolution? That was it. The audience was now his for the taking. The Experience pushed on through "Rock Me Baby"—with Hendrix first giving the crowd a demonstration of how bluesman B.B. King might have played it before blasting through his own version. The band followed with "Can You See Me?," "Hey Joe," "The Wind Cries Mary," and "Purple Haze."

With each successive song, the intensity increased, building toward the grand finale. When the set was nearly finished, Hendrix addressed the crowd for a final time:

> Man, it's so groovy to come back here this way and, you know, really get a chance to really play.... I can sit here all night and say thank you, thank you, thank you,

but I could just as well grab you, man—but I just can't do that ... so what I'm gonna do is sacrifice something here that I really love, OK.... Don't think I'm silly doing this 'cause I don't think I'm losing my mind.... There's nothing more I can do than this.

As Hendrix whipped into "Wild Thing" by the Troggs, his guitar shrieked, as if the devil were trying to drag it into hell. He had sworn that he was going to pull out all the stops, and did he ever, playing his guitar between his legs, with his teeth, on his knees, behind his back—all the while going for maximum feedback and frenzy. As the final chords rang through the air, Hendrix grabbed something at the back of the stage, then came forward again. Out came a can of lighter fluid and matches. After giving a scorching musical performance, he set his Stratocaster ablaze.

Grabbing the still-burning instrument, he smashed it, then threw the blackened, splintered pieces into the crowd and walked off the stage. The sacrifice was done. The voodoo had worked. Jimi Hendrix—a poor black kid from Seattle who had grown up playing air guitar with a broom—had come to the Monterey International Pop Festival as basically a musical unknown. He was leaving it a rock legend.

2

A Legend's Roots

From the very start, the man whom the world would come to know as Jimi Hendrix had an unconventional, unpredictable life, the latest in a long line of Hendrixes—blacks, Cherokees, and whites among them—who would lead a gypsy existence. Also like his ancestors, music would be an ingrained part of his being.

Johnny Allen Hendrix was born on November 27, 1942, in Seattle, Washington, to parents who were ill-prepared for his arrival into their world. His mother, Lucille Jeter, was a junior-high dropout who was barely 17; his father, Al Hendrix, was a fitfully employed unskilled laborer. About all they had in common was their mutual love of dancing and music.

Al's passion for dance came from his mother, Nora Moore. She had spent years as a chorus girl with various traveling vaudeville troupes that zigzagged across the country during the early twentieth century, living out of suitcases and stopping wherever a paying audience could be found. While performing in one troupe, she met her husband, Bertran Philander Ross Hendrix, who was working as a stagehand with the company. In 1911, their troupe hit Seattle, where it went broke and disbanded. Stranded, and having had enough of the gypsy way of life anyway, the Hendrixes decided to settle in the Pacific Northwest. The couple heard that work could be found across the gray waters of Puget Sound in Vancouver, and so they moved to Canada. Ross got a job working as a steward at a Vancouver golf club.

Nora and Ross Hendrix had four children between 1913 and 1919. The youngest, James Allen, known as Al, was a small but muscular youth who had inherited not only his mother's love of dancing but also his father's skill at self-defense, occasionally boxing as a lightweight at a local club. His father died when Al was just 15, and the family was forced to go on welfare. Al soon dropped out of high school, hoping to make it in show business as a dancer. But it was the height of the Great Depression, and jobs and money were scarce—especially for blacks. Still, Al kept his spirits up by entering dance contests, which he often won with his complicated, acrobatic moves. Then, around 1936, a friend told him about a chance to box for money down in Seattle. The boxing opportunity turned out to be a sham, and Al returned to Vancouver. But finding a steady job there proved elusive. Deciding that he would have a better chance of getting work in Seattle—and the larger black population made it more likely that he would find a girlfriend—he reversed his parents' path. In 1940, he returned to Seattle for good with $40 to his name.

MAGIC ON THE DANCE FLOOR

Even during the Depression, Seattle was a place with possibilities. The rain-shrouded city had graduated from logging—its original source of wealth—to steel, shipbuilding, and aircraft manufacturing. Al started out working odd jobs, but he was persistent and strong, and he eventually got a decent-paying job at an iron foundry. It was back-breaking work, but at the end of the day he would put on his brown pinstriped zoot suit and hit the nightclubs, where he came alive on the dance floor. He was working at the foundry when he met Lucille Jeter.

A beautiful, naive ninth grader who lived to go dancing, Lucille had stopped at a friend's house on her way to a dance. The house happened to be the boardinghouse where Al lived. The friend happened to be his landlady's daughter, who introduced Lucille to the older man. When Lucille mentioned where she was headed, Al suggested they go together. The delicate, pale-skinned Lucille looked too frail to be all that energetic, but she was "a jitterbugging whirlwind" of a dancer. The schoolgirl and the laborer made an odd-looking pair, but that night they discovered they were magical on the dance floor. Al Hendrix had found the partner of his dreams. They started dating regularly, although her parents did not take the relationship too seriously because their daughter was so young. Lucille had just turned 16; Al was 22.

On December 7, 1941, Japanese forces carried out a devastating surprise attack on the U.S. military base at Pearl Harbor in Hawaii, plunging the United States into World War II. As frequently happens during wartime, many relationships moved faster than they normally would have. Fearing that he would soon be drafted into the army, Al sped up his courtship. His fears were realized when he received his draft notice early in 1942. Around the same time, Lucille found that she was pregnant. Although Al immediately proposed marriage, Lucille's parents were furious. They wanted more for their beautiful young daughter than a shotgun marriage to a man she barely knew. But Al prevailed, and on March 31, 1942, they got married. Three days later, Al reported for duty. He and Lucille never even had the chance to live together.

Lucille, meanwhile, had dropped out of school and was living at home with her disapproving parents. She managed to find a job as a waitress at a club on Jackson Street, a sleazy area notorious for gambling, prostitution, and drugs. But it was also where the best R&B in Seattle could be heard, and that milieu was right up Lucille's alley. It was a world that she would gravitate to for the rest of her short life.

BIRTH

By late summer, Lucille's pregnancy prevented her from continuing in her job, and she moved in with a family friend, Dorothy Harding. On November 27, 1942, Lucille gave birth to a son in King County Hospital in Seattle. She named him Johnny Allen Hendrix. Her family nicknamed him Buster.

Al Hendrix, who was stationed in Alabama, had requested a furlough for the birth of his child, which was permitted under army regulations. Not only was he refused—being told that Seattle was too far to travel there and back in the few days allotted—he was immediately thrown into the stockade for a month and a half. He suspected that he was locked up to keep from going AWOL, but his sergeant simply said it was on "general principles." Al was finally sent to fight in the Pacific Front: the Fiji Islands, New Guinea, and Guadalcanal. Other than a few photos, he would not see his son until the end of the war. Making matters worse, Lucille's letters became more and more infrequent—usually with a different return address from the last time—and the ones he sent to her were often sent back as undeliverable.

Meanwhile, Lucille was having a hard time with young motherhood and often left her infant son in the care of her mother, her sister, or friends. She was recklessly determined to pursue the more interesting pleasures that life had to offer a teenage girl—especially nightclubs and dance halls. Lucille's mother, Clarice Jeter, cleaned house for her good friend Minnie Gautier and Minnie's daughter, Freddie Mae. In *Electric Gypsy*, Freddie Mae told how Clarice had shown up one snowy day in early December, carrying a bundle. When Clarice came in the door, "[she] had this baby in her arms, about two weeks old, with its little legs sticking out ... and the baby's legs were just blue." Clarice explained that the baby was Lucille's and that she had not seen her daughter in several days "and so she had to bring him.... I remember [my mother] going on at Mrs. Jeter because she and Lucille lived clear across town ... yet Mrs. Jeter had just brought him in a little blanket. He had wet so much and it was so cold that the diaper had frozen, and ... Mrs. Jeter had no diapers or bottle." Minnie insisted that Clarice leave the child with her until Lucille came for him. She finally did—a month or two later. "When she did come, my mother told her, 'It's a shame to leave this baby with your mother, and I'm gonna ... keep him.' And Lucille said, 'OK.' It wasn't any big deal for her."

By then, Lucille was drinking heavily and running around— she was not the type to sit patiently at home and wait for her husband to return from war. She hooked up with an unsavory man named John Page (or John Williams, according to some sources), who hauled her—and sometimes her baby—from one seedy hotel and rooming house to another. Little Johnny Allen was forced into the gypsy way of life from the get-go, shunted from his mother, to a relative, to a friend, and back in a never-ending cycle.

In 1945, as the war was winding down, Al Hendrix received a letter telling him that his now three-year-old son had been left in the care of a Mrs. Champ, a new friend of his mother-in-law's in Berkeley, California. Clarice had met her while attending a church convention there. Al had also gotten wind of his wife's behavior and started divorce proceedings. But when Al was finally discharged and retrieved his son and brought him home to Seattle, he dropped the divorce suit and reconciled with Lucille. He also legally changed his son's name to James Marshall Hendrix, not wanting his son to grow up with a name similar to the man who had been Lucille's lover. Johnny was now Jimmy.

The Family Tree

The family history and lineage of Jimi Hendrix is rich and complex. On his maternal side, his grandfather, Preston Jeter, was the son of a former slave and her slave master. Born in 1875 in Richmond, Virginia, Preston worked in the coal mines around Charleston until he witnessed a lynching and fled north to Boston. There, a white doctor befriended him and even put him through college. His education did not help him find a job, however, and Preston decided to strike out for the Northwest, where life was supposedly better for blacks. That turned out not to be the case, but there he met and married Clarice Lawson. Originally from Little Rock, Arkansas, her ancestral tree included black slaves and Cherokees. Preston worked in the coal mines, and Clarice cleaned houses. The couple eventually had eight children—Jimi's mother, Lucille, was the youngest. Life was tough for a black family with so many children and few decent job opportunities, and the children occasionally had to be sent to foster homes.

Jimi's paternal side was even more colorful and varied. His great-great-grandparents were a full-blooded Native American woman and an Irishman. Back in the 1830s the Cherokee had what white pioneers wanted: land. They were forced off their ancestral homeland by a fraudulent treaty that handed over 7 million acres to the state of Georgia. Some 17,000 Cherokee were forcibly removed by U.S. soldiers and marched across the country to Oklahoma on what came to be known as the Trail of Tears. Nearly a third of the people died along the way of cold, starvation, disease, and just plain exhaustion. About 1,000 Cherokee fled into the mountains, however. One of them was a Cherokee princess who married an Irishman named Moore. Their son, Robert, married a black woman named Fanny. Robert and Fanny's daughter, Nora, was Jimi's paternal grandmother.

Jimi's paternal grandfather, Bertran Philander Ross Hendrix, was born in Urbana, Ohio, the son of a poor light-skinned black woman named Fanny Hendrix and her wealthy white employer, Bertran Philander Ross—likely the result of either rape or seduction. She boldly named him after his father, though it did Ross, as he was called, no good. He left home and headed to Chicago, where he was employed as a constable. After a while he hit the road again and joined a vaudeville troupe as a stagehand—there met and married Nora Moore. They had four sons—Al Hendrix, Jimi's father, was the youngest.

The two branches of Jimi Hendrix's family tree passed on an unending restlessness and an ingrained love of music to the scion who would blaze briefly like a fiery comet before burning himself out at the age of 27.

UNSETTLED HOME LIFE

Even after the family was reunited, Jimmy's home life remained unstable. To save on expenses, Al, Lucille, and Jimmy moved in with Lucille's sister Delores and her two children. Al and Lucille, though, began drinking heavily, and after a while, Delores—tired of baby-sitting while they went out and partied every night—threw them out. Al struggled to make a living, and Lucille struggled to accept the burdens of family life.

A steady pattern emerged: They would fight, separate, and reconcile; fight, separate, and reconcile. In January 1948, Lucille gave birth to a second son, Leon. But it seemed impossible for her to give up her old wandering ways. Although she was a loving mother when she was around, she often abandoned her sons and left their care to her husband, who was working days at menial jobs while he studied to be an electrician under the G.I. Bill. Quoted in *Electric Gypsy*, Leon noted that his mother "would give us all the love she had for a few days, then she'd be gone for a few months." Another son was born just 11 months after Leon, in November 1948. Al named him Joseph Allan Hendrix, although he would later deny paternity. Joe was born with many birth defects—a likely result of Lucille's heavy drinking—which required extensive medical care. Then in 1950 Lucille gave birth to a daughter, Cathy, born four months premature and blind, and, in 1951, another daughter, Pamela, also was born with health problems. Both girls—likely fathered by other men, although Al's name is on their birth certificates—were soon given up for adoption.

Finally, with rancor having built a wall between them, Lucille and Al officially divorced on December 17, 1951. It wasn't long, though, before the old push-pull between them came into play again, and they moved back in together. The reconciliation didn't stick, prodded by Al's refusal to pay for Joe's medical care and his insistence that the boy be made a ward of the state to get all his medical expenses covered. In the summer of 1952, Al borrowed a car and drove Joe to a hospital, where Lucille handed over the weeping three-year-old to a nurse. He would never see his mother again. The following Valentine's Day, Lucille gave birth to yet another child, her fourth with birth defects—a developmentally disabled boy named Alfred who was immediately put up for adoption.

Although Al had been awarded custody of his sons in the divorce, the de facto parenting was left to others. Jimmy was cared for by a succession of relatives and family friends, moving through a series of houses, apartments, and rented rooms and bouncing from school to school. For a while he lived with his aunt Pat and his grandmother Nora in Vancouver. He loved to hear his grandmother's tales of her vaudeville days and her Cherokee ancestry. "My grandmother used to tell me beautiful Indian stories," Hendrix said in a 1967 interview. "I used to see her a lot, you know, and she used to make these clothes for me.... I used to go back [to Seattle] and take these clothes to school and wear them and all that, and you know, people would laugh."

Al was unable to get a good job and often lost the mediocre ones that he did get. His own out-all-night drinking and gambling habits certainly did not sustain any kind of constancy for his boys, who often relied on the kindness of relatives and neighbors to feed and house them. The family's instability drew the scrutiny of social workers. At 12, Jimmy was old enough to better fend for himself and was left under his father's care, but Leon was placed in a series of foster homes. Al often took Jimmy to the homes of various friends and relatives who would care for him until Al was able to take him back. Sometimes father and son could only be together on weekends, when Al would occasionally take Jimmy and Leon to the movies. Jimmy's favorites were the *Flash Gordon* serials, which spurred a passion for science fiction that would later reveal itself in his music.

Not surprisingly, all the disorder and insecurity in his life sent Jimmy retreating inward. He found comfort and stability in his own private world and was unwilling to form any kind of emotional attachments, since they always ended painfully. "This pinball existence ... made him ultimately aloof and fearful of emotional commitment—an attitude sometimes rationalized by the adult Jimi as 'freedom,' " Harry Shapiro and Caesar Glebbeek wrote in *Jimi Hendrix: Electric Gypsy*. A shy, imaginative kid, he wrote stories and drew pictures, constructing a vivid universe of planets and stars. One of the few school subjects to hold his interest was art. Oddly enough, he actually did poorly in music class, although, like his parents, he loved music and grew up listening to his father's collection of records by Muddy Waters, T-Bone Walker, and other blues greats. "The first guitarist I was aware of was Muddy Waters," he later recalled. "I heard one of his old records when I was a little boy, and it scared me to death."

He was also a whiz at broom guitar—playing so energetically that the broom would lose its straw. Recalled Leon Hendrix in *Room Full of Mirrors*, "Dad, he'd come in yellin' and screamin', veins poppin' out of his forehead. 'Brooms cost money!' ... But [Jimmy] kept right on singing the notes and pretending to play. He'd walk down the street with the broom, even take it to school. Everyone thought he was crazy." From the broom, he moved on to a cigar box with a hole cut out of it and a string stretched across the middle. Then he got a one-string ukulele that Al found when he was hired to clean out a garage. Jimmy, however, longed for a real guitar.

Jimmy's home life continued to decline. His father had lost yet another job, and their house was deteriorating into squalor—at one point the electricity was cut off—forcing them to move into a boardinghouse. Jimmy wandered the neighborhood, often stopping to listen to musicians when he heard someone playing. Finally when he was 15, he got his first real guitar. One account says that he got the instrument from their landlady's son for five dollars; others have a gambling buddy of Al's selling it for the same five dollars. All accounts

Blues musician Muddy Waters is shown in a photograph from the 1950s. Listening to his father's record collection, young Jimmy Hendrix heard musicians like Waters and T-Bone Walker. Hendrix would later incorporate several of Waters's classic songs into his repertoire.

agree that Al very reluctantly paid for the instrument and only did so after a family friend berated him. Despite Al's insistence that he play it right-handed—"My dad thought everything left-handed was from the devil," Leon told biographer Charles R. Cross—Jimmy restrung the guitar backward so that he could play it left-handed. To him, it felt more natural when he used his right hand on the neck. He figured out the tuning by going to a music store and running his fingers on a guitar there. "After that I was able to tune my own," he later recalled. Jimmy was so thrilled with his new guitar that he barely let it out of his sight or his hands.

A TERRIBLE LOSS

That same year, 1958, Jimmy faced the greatest sadness of his young life: On February 1, Lucille Hendrix died. She was only 32. Although she and Al had long been divorced—and although she had even remarried a month earlier to a much older retired longshoreman—they continued to get together whenever they ran into each other at their favorite tavern. She had twice been hospitalized for cirrhosis of the liver during the previous few months and was hospitalized again in mid-January with hepatitis. Her ill health affected her beauty and her outlook, and she had told her sister Delores that she was not going to live long. Delores tried to convince her otherwise, but barely a week later, Lucille was found unconscious in the alley beside the tavern she frequented. Admitted to the hospital yet again, she was dead a few hours later from a ruptured spleen. It was never determined what kind of trauma might have caused the rupture—whether a fall or a blow. Added to the boys' shock was their father's refusal to let them attend their mother's funeral. Neither Jimmy nor Leon ever forgave their father for not letting them say good-bye to their mother.

Jimmy internalized his sadness and buried his grief over his mother's death by becoming even more obsessed with playing his guitar. The instrument essentially defined who he was, and for the first time he found the self-esteem that had eluded him his whole life. "The guitar was to be his place in the world, his voice.... It was his talent as a musician that gave Jimmy a measure of self-confidence rarely found in somebody with his kind of disrupted background," Shapiro and Glebbeek wrote in *Electric Gypsy*.

He played day and night, absorbing all he could from records and the radio, schooling himself in the blues artistry of B.B. King, Muddy Waters, John Lee Hooker, and Elmore James. He began skipping school to hang out with the neighborhood musicians, sneaking into clubs to watch others play, and then going home and practicing their licks, the notes, the chords,

As Jimmy Hendrix was growing up, another influence was rock guitarist Chuck Berry, shown here during a 1955 performance. Hendrix liked the way the guitar drove songs like Berry's "Johnny B. Goode."

over and over until he mastered them. Jimmy was especially thrilled with the hot new sound that a New York DJ named Alan Freed had christened "rock and roll." He loved the way the guitars drove Eddie Cochran's "Summertime Blues" and Chuck Berry's "Johnny B. Goode." He loved the frenzy Elvis Presley whipped up with his voice on "That's All Right Mama" and "Jailhouse Rock."

When he turned 16, Jimmy began longing for an *electric* guitar. Leon recalled how Jimmy had tried to electrify his acoustic guitar by rewiring the family stereo. The same family friend who had chastised Al into buying Jimmy his five-dollar acoustic now badgered him to buy his son an electric guitar. Al eventually gave in and purchased one on an installment plan from the local music store. The white Supro Ozark might have been a bushel of diamonds for all the pleasure it gave Jimmy. According to Carmen Goudy, his girlfriend at the time, Jimmy literally jumped for joy. "I think it was the happiest day of his life." Jimmy did not have an amplifier to plug his guitar into, but that did not seem to bother him. Occasionally, he did get to hook up to the amps of one of his older musician friends or the amp at the Rotary Boys' Club, where anyone was allowed to practice— even those playing rock and roll.

JOINING A BAND

Now that Jimmy had a real electric guitar, he was virtually unstoppable. He learned songs so quickly that his good friend and fellow musician Jimmy Williams called him "a human jukebox." He also played with a lot of flash—too much at times. His over-the-top style got him bounced from his first band try-out. But in the summer of 1959, Jimmy joined a band formed by a group of high-school friends, the Velvetones. Jimmy especially enjoyed the instrumental tunes—"Honky Tonk," by Bill Doggett, "Rebel Rouser," by Duane Eddy, and the "Peter Gunn Theme" by Henry Mancini, whose locomotive bass-guitar riff Jimmy loved. The Velvetones landed a regular gig on teenage dance nights at a Seattle club called Birdland, where one night someone stole Jimmy's guitar. Jimmy was afraid to tell his father—when Al got in a rage, he would beat his son. When Jimmy finally summoned the courage to tell Al what had happened, Jimmy got severely reprimanded, but he also got a new guitar. The stolen Supro was replaced with a white

IN HIS OWN WORDS...

Jimi Hendrix recalled in an interview with *Beat Instrumental* in 1967 how he had found his path in life and stuck with it:

> When I was 15, I decided the guitar was the instrument for me. Then I got tired of the guitar and put it aside, but when I heard Chuck Berry, it revived my interest. I learned all the riffs I could.

Danelectro that Jimmy painted red. He also joined a new band, the Rocking Kings, which even had a manager, James Thomas. Jimmy was soon playing gigs all over the Seattle area.

The Rocking Kings performed at private parties, social clubs, and dance halls throughout 1959 and 1960, playing such hits as "Searchin'" and "Yakety Yak" by the Coasters, "At the Hop" by Danny and the Juniors, and "The Twist" by Hank Ballard. As Jimmy recalled in the February 22, 1969, issue of the weekly *Melody Maker,* "In those days I just liked rock and roll, I guess. We used to have to play stuff by people like the Coasters. Anyway, you all had to do the same things before you could join a band— you all even had to do the same steps." To give them a more professional look, the band's manager insisted that they wear sports jackets; Jimmy remembered one gig where the jacket rental cost more than the money he earned that night.

The Rocking Kings gradually built a following, and, in 1960, the group took second place in the All-State Band of the Year tournament held in Seattle. During that time, Jimmy was also gigging with other bands. Leon Hendrix recalled in *Black Gold,* "Jimmy would walk right across town if somebody said he could probably play there." He also started to experiment with different sounds—and a different look—getting bored with repeating the same old riffs and moves night after night.

Like most bands, the Rocking Kings eventually ran out of steam and changed directions. A few members quit. Jimmy stayed on but switched from bass to lead guitar. Manager James Thomas called the new combo Thomas and the Tomcats, after himself. Jimmy devoted a great deal of energy to the revamped band—he was playing and rehearsing nearly all the time—and his school atten- dance suffered. He started to get warning letters that told him he would be expelled if he did not show up for class. By the end of October 1960, Jimmy was officially finished with school. Although he would tell people he quit because he felt he had learned all he could and was ready for a taste of the real world, the simpler truth is that Jimmy Hendrix flunked out.

Al Hendrix had started a gardening business, and Jimmy worked for his father for a while. He hated working for his father—who treated him badly and paid him even worse—and he soon became restless. Unfortunately, his taste for adventure sometimes got him in trouble. One night, he and a group of buddies broke into a department store and stole some clothes. The next day, though, either out of remorse or fear of being caught, they tossed the clothes into a bin for the needy (even though Jimmy himself could have qualified on that score). They were found out anyway, but the store decided not to press charges in exchange for gardening services from Al. Then, in May 1961, Jimmy was arrested while joyriding with friends in a stolen car. The judge gave him a choice: a two-year sentence or a two-year suspended sentence if he joined the army.

As an 18-year-old high-school dropout with a criminal record, Jimmy would have few job prospects. He had no problem with the army because he always had strong patriotic feelings, and the Cold War was still raging; in fact, not long before, he had visited the local Air Force recruitment office. But black pilots were a rarity then, and Jimmy was turned down—on the grounds of not having sufficient physical endurance. Now, facing jail time or the army, he gratefully opted for the latter. He hoped to become a paratrooper with the 101st Airborne Division. Being a paratrooper required enlisting for a three-year hitch.

On May 28, 1961, Jimmy played his last gig with Thomas and the Tomcats: an outdoor street festival and dance. Jimmy had a steady girlfriend, Betty Jean Morgan, and that night he gave her an "engagement ring"—a cheap rhinestone. Probably more important to Jimmy, he got from her a promise to keep his guitar at her house for safekeeping. On May 31, 1961, Jimmy Hendrix arrived by train at Fort Ord, California, for basic training with the United States Army. He was now recruit #RA 19 693 532.

3

Little Wing

Jimi Hendrix would later insist that he "hated the army immediately," and, temperamentally, he appears to have been spectacularly unsuited for army life. At first, though, it seemed to suit him well. Perhaps because it was so antithetical to his unstructured upbringing, Hendrix initially found the predictability of army life and being told what to do and when to do it comforting. His biggest complaints were pretty minor, according to a letter he wrote to his father on June 8: "All, I mean ALL my hair's cut off, and I have to shave." He also asked to borrow some money because he would not be getting paid until the end of the month. One thing was very evident in his letters: He was homesick. One other thing was very evident from his letters to and from Al: He and his father were getting along better than they ever had.

Hendrix completed his basic training on August 4, 1961. He was now Private James Hendrix. A month later, he got a one-week furlough to go home, where—looking proud in his dress uniform—he had emotional reunions with Al, Leon, and Betty Jean. Then it was back to Fort Ord to await his permanent assignment. At the end of October, he finally got his assignment. He also got his wish: He would be a supply clerk at Fort Campbell, Kentucky, home of the 101st Airborne, known as the Screaming Eagles paratroop division. Hendrix's dream to earn the distinctive sleeve patch worn by the men of the high-flying 101st looked as if it would become a reality.

He arrived at Fort Campbell on November 8. A few days later, he wrote to his father:

> Well, here I am, exactly where I wanted to go in the 101st Airborne. We jumped out of a 34-foot tower on the third day we were here. It was almost fun.... There were three guys who quit when they got to the top of the tower.... They took one look outside and just quit. And that got me thinking as I was walking up those steps, but I made up my mind that whatever happens, I'm not quitting on my own.... They work you to DEATH, fussing and fighting ... and half the people quit then, too. That's how they separate the men from the boys. I pray that I will make it on the men's side this time.

On his first simulated jump, Hendrix landed hard in a sand dune, but he was eager to try it again. He was also eager to try the real thing. The notion of flight was intoxicating to a young man who daydreamed about the heavens and the cosmos. He wanted to experience the sensation of an aircraft lifting him up. He wanted to breathe the air a mile above the earth and briefly exist in that endless blue space, with the ground spread out like a blanket waiting to catch him.

He learned quickly at Fort Campbell and was jumping out of airplanes within weeks. At times he would board the craft with a camera and take pictures while falling. He included these

In 1960, soldiers from the 101st Airborne Division trained at Fort Campbell in Kentucky. Jimmy Hendrix's dream of wearing the sleeve patch
of the 101st seemed closer when he was stationed at Fort Campbell in
1961. He and the army, however, were not a well-suited match.

aerial snapshots in his frequent letters home. "It's just as much fun as it looks," read the note on the back of one he sent to his father, "if you keep your eyes open (smile)."

MILITARY MUSICIANS

Hendrix also made a good friend at Fort Campbell, a fellow soldier named Billy Cox. Cox came from a musical family—his mother was a classical pianist and his uncle played sax with Duke Ellington's orchestra—and he was an upright bass player. Like Hendrix, he had played with a number of bands before joining the army. One day, he happened by a practice room on the base, where Hendrix was playing a borrowed guitar. Cox introduced himself and checked out a bass. That was that. The two became instant buddies and began to jam regularly.

In January 1962, eight months into his army career, Jimmy Hendrix wrote home to ask for his Danelectro—he was tired of playing on army-issue guitars. His father carefully wrapped and mailed it. Once the red Danelectro was back in his hands, he rarely let it out of his sight and played the instrument whenever he had a free moment. Some nights, he fell asleep in his bunk with the guitar still in his hands.

It was at this time that the army began to wash its hands of Private James M. Hendrix. According to Hendrix's army records (as uncovered by *The Smoking Gun* Website), his first lieutenant began an investigation to have Hendrix dismissed from the army. On January 4, 1962, Sergeant Billy Bowman wrote a statement, as requested by his commanding officer, Lieutenant William Potts. It said that when Hendrix was assigned to his squad, he "started out showing lack of interest in his equipment and his work in the section." Despite repeated counseling, the statement continued:

> Pvt Hendrix showed no interest. Constant supervision is necessary to keep Pvt Hendrix from making minor mistakes about which he has been told time after time.

On many occasions Pvt Hendrix has been found sleeping on the job. Pvt Hendrix on many occasions has missed bed check.... In my opinion Pvt Hendrix should be eliminated from the service.

While the military gears slowly ground on, Hendrix and Cox formed a band with several fellow soldiers and began playing on weekends at venues on the base. The band also played at a nearby club, the Pink Poodle, just over the border in Clarksville, Tennessee. Stationed as he was in the South, Hendrix had his first real taste of Jim Crow segregation, and the Pink Poodle was the place where black servicemen hung out. There, Hendrix also received an education in Southern blues and the blues greats from the region. His band went through various lineups and eventually settled in with five instrumentalists (two guitars, a bass, drums, and a saxophone) plus a vocalist—"Jimmy was too timid to sing, and they laughed at me when *I* sang," Cox told Stephen Roby in *Black Gold.* They called themselves the King Kasuals.

Hendrix started sending U.S. savings bonds to Betty Jean Morgan with his letters. He also talked repeatedly of marriage and even sent her an engagement ring with a real diamond. Just a few months later, however, he seemed more interested in his band than anything else in his life. When its members were not on duty, the King Kasuals played weekend gigs off base, traveling as far as North Carolina. Usually they covered songs by popular artists, like "Quarter to Three" by Gary "U.S." Bonds and "Tossin' and Turnin'" by Bobby Lewis. Hendrix developed a small but devoted following among clubgoers and guitar players in the area around Fort Campbell. He also met a number of women who were more than a little interested in the handsome, flamboyant musician.

THE ARMY'S COMPLAINTS

Now the army added Hendrix's distraction with his music—and an unpaid laundry bill—to its list of complaints.

On May 24, Hendrix's platoon sergeant, James C. Spears, attested to the following:

> Pvt Hendrix for approximately 6 months.... This individual has shown very little interest in the Army, his personal equipment, and his area in the billets.... Numerous attempts at counseling by his platoon leader, section leader, section chief, and myself on his ability to become a better soldier have met with negative results.... Pvt Hendrix fails to pay just debts. He owes a laundry bill of approximately $80.00 and has made no effort whatsoever to pay it.... He said he had given the money to a buddy in an infantry unit to pay this debt for him. It was later proven he had lied about this.... Pvt Hendrix plays a musical instrument in a band off duty and has let this interfere with his military duties in so much as missing bed check and not getting enough sleep. He has no interest whatsoever in the Army.... It is my opinion that Pvt Hendrix will never come up to the standards required of a soldier. I feel that the military service will benefit if he is discharged ... as soon as possible.

Hendrix's section leader, a second lieutenant, wrote a corroborating letter on June 1, in which he, too, stated, "I believe that Pvt Hendrix should be eliminated from the service."

His commanding officer then requested that the young soldier be examined by a psychiatrist for his repeated disciplinary problems. Captain Gilbert Batchman recommended the examination because he had received complaints from Hendrix's first sergeant, his platoon leader, and his section sergeants—as well as several fellow soldiers—that Hendrix was "unable to conform to military rules and regulations. Misses bed check; sleeps while supposed to be working; unsatisfactory duty performance. Requires excessive supervision at all times.... He appears to be an extreme introvert.... This man has the same type problems under two squad leaders. Performance of duty in the barracks and as a supply clerk is unsatisfactory under both supervisors."

On May 28, another sergeant, Louis Hoekstra, added his voice to the growing chorus:

> Hendrix is poorly motivated for the military.... Hendrix has been counseled regarding his shortcomings at extreme lengths by Capt Gilbert R Batchman, to no avail. At times Hendrix isn't able to carry on an intelligent conversation.... At one point it was thought perhaps Hendrix was taking dope.... He has been undergoing group therapy at Mental Hygeine [sic] with negative results. Pvt Hendrix plays a musical instrument during his off duty hours, or so he says. This is one of his faults, because his mind apparently cannot function while performing duties and thinking about his guitar.... I recommend without hesitancy that Hendrix be eliminated from the service under the provisions of AR 635-208 as expeditious as possible.

The army—and apparently Jimmy Hendrix—got its wish. On May 31, 1962, a Request for Discharge was sent to the commanding officer of the 101st Airborne Support Group, 101st Airborne Division, recommending that, because of his "behavior problems," Hendrix, James M., RA 19 693 532, Pvt E-2, receive an "undesirable" discharge. Hendrix then initialed a statement testifying that he had been counseled about the recommended action, that he had read the statements that supported his commanding officer's discharge recommendation, and that he requested neither a hearing nor "a desire to submit a statement in my behalf." And so, with the signature of "Larry Gantt, 1st Lieutenant Shop Officer" and the countersignature of "James M. Hendrix, PVT," Jimmy Hendrix's army career came to an abrupt end.

Family members always maintained that Hendrix's letters invariably expressed his pride in being a Screaming Eagle and that he had no desire to leave the army. By contrast, Hendrix's biographers have stated that army authority rankled him and that he especially resented not being able to play when and where he wanted. All, however, had maintained that Hendrix's break from the army was due to a *literal* break—a broken ankle. Hendrix's army files say nothing about a broken bone but instead make clear that the army did not want him any more than he, apparently, wanted the army.

In any event, Jimmy Hendrix left Fort Campbell in July 1962. His plan was to stick around the area until Billy Cox was discharged in a couple of months, and then the two of them would strike out to become professional musicians. Although Hendrix had planned on going home to Seattle to see Betty Jean, that idea changed when he met a local woman named Joyce Lucas. He wrote Betty Jean and told her that he would not be returning to Seattle, and she gave back the engagement ring. When Cox was discharged, he, Hendrix, Joyce Lucas and another couple all rented a small house together. The arrangement lasted a few months until Hendrix and Cox put together a new version of the King Kasuals, which was soon hired by the Del Morocco club in Nashville, Tennessee.

PLAYING IN NASHVILLE
In 1962, Nashville had a budding rhythm-and-blues scene. The Kasuals started playing at more Nashville clubs but for very little money. Hendrix and Cox often depended on friends or nightclub managers for basics like food and shelter. Hendrix was good-looking, talented, and charming—a magnet for the ladies. He had an unofficial fan club of young women who called themselves the Buttons because they sewed and mended his stage clothes. Still, however interested Hendrix was in women, he was more interested in perfecting his craft. In a town full of gifted musicians, where the skill level was high and

competition was fierce, Jimmy Hendrix began to carve out a reputation as a serious player.

He also met and became friends with guitarist Larry Lee in Nashville. Hendrix, Cox, and Lee would one day share the stage at the Woodstock festival, but in Nashville they were just poor, hopeful musicians, hanging out and jamming together, sleeping under other people's roofs. Nashville was Hendrix's early proving ground. "In the bars I used to play in," he later said, "you really had to play, 'cause those people were really hard to please. It was one of the hardest audiences in the South; they hear it all the time. Everybody knows how to play guitar. You went down the street and people are sitting on their porch playing more guitar. That's where I learned to play, really, in Nashville."

Hendrix tried to find work as a session player—musicians hired to back up recording artists—but his one attempt would also be his last. His sound was just too bizarre for the producer, who actually cut Hendrix's track off of the recording. He briefly found work on a package tour with the Marvellettes and Curtis Mayfield, although Mayfield banished Hendrix from the stage whenever he himself played, finding Hendrix's playing just too wild.

IN HIS OWN WORDS...

Jimi Hendrix is famous for playing guitar in unconventional ways. Hendrix's audiences came to his concerts for his flamboyant showmanship as much as his music. Aside from playing his guitar above his head, behind his back, and between his legs, Hendrix was able to play the strings with his teeth. It was something that he learned in his early days of playing. *Electric Gypsy* quoted a 1969 interview in which Hendrix explained how he came to play with his teeth:

> The idea of doing that came to me in a town in Tennessee. Down there you have to play with your teeth or else you get shot. There's a trail of broken teeth all over the stage.

Late that winter, with little work coming his way, Hendrix decided to take a break and, borrowing the bus fare, he headed up to Vancouver to stay with his grandmother Nora. In Vancouver, Hendrix hooked up for a few weekend gigs with an R&B group called Bobby Taylor and the Vancouvers. The group featured Tommy Chong, later of Cheech and Chong fame, on guitar. In the spring of 1963, Hendrix returned to Nashville. There he joined what was known as the Chitlin' Circuit, named for a Southern soul-food delicacy. The Chitlin' Circuit was a string of music venues—clubs, bars, and theaters—where black R&B and blues musicians could play for their fans and hope for wider exposure; they received virtually no air play on white-owned radio stations. Hendrix joined a package tour that featured Sam Cooke and Jackie Wilson, two leading artists whose styles combined soul music with rhythm and blues. The tour promoter was George Odell, more of a showman than a musician, who wore an outrageous silver wig and clothes that were even louder than the music. Cox was wary of the self-promoter and opted out, but Hendrix jumped aboard Odell's tour bus for a ride that would carry him, on and off, through the next two years. Traveling the country, Hendrix played behind some of the top pop acts of the day. Aside from Cooke and Wilson, Jimmy backed up Curtis Mayfield, Hank Ballard and the Midnighters, Solomon Burke, and later, Little Richard. As Charles Cross noted in *Room Full of Mirrors,* "Hendrix soon felt as though he had seen the inside of every juke joint and tavern from Virginia to Florida to Texas.... [Yet the tour offered] Jimi invaluable lessons in showmanship, audience interaction, and survival as a touring musician."

On the road, Hendrix encountered some of the guitar heroes who had influenced his playing. During a visit to Chess Records, home of the Chicago blues, he met Muddy Waters, the first guitarist he ever remembered hearing, and they spent an afternoon talking about guitar and trading secrets. Later in his career, Hendrix would incorporate a number of the bluesman's classic songs into his repertoire, adapting them to his own style. For now, though, it was enough for him to realize that he could hold his own with the musicians he had admired as a kid. It also, as biographer Cross noted, "helped cement his growing sense that playing in a Nashville cover band was not his fate."

ON TO NEW YORK

In late 1963, a promoter from New York caught Jimmy Hendrix playing in Nashville and convinced him that he would become a star in the Big Apple. Hendrix took the bait. He tried to get his bandmates to go with him, but Cox believed that the King Kasuals would soon hit it big in Nashville, and their other guitarist was put off by Hendrix's growing dependency on amphetamines. So Hendrix boarded a Greyhound bus—guitar slung over his back as always—and chased his dream to New York.

Once there, he headed uptown to Harlem, the cultural and spiritual center of New York's African-American community. Though he was a seasoned traveler, nothing could have prepared him for Harlem in the 1960s. The tangle of grit, menace, attitude, and raw energy was unlike anything the young man from faraway Seattle had ever experienced. As usual, Hendrix was penniless upon arrival and had to pawn his guitar for food and hotel money. (The guitar was often in and out of the pawnshop, redeemed and then hocked for cash again.) Gigs turned out to be hard to come by, and he took whatever he could find, including playing in the background for a stripper. Some nights he had to sleep in an alley or pick through trash cans for food. During the day, he would hang around recording studios or Harlem clubs like the Palm Café, checking out the local musicians and trying to get invited to play with house bands. It was rough going. Despite Hendrix's talents and his résumé, the established players shrugged him off. But his confidence was not shaken. He entered the talent competition at Harlem's legendary Apollo Theater one night and won first prize—$25. Unfortunately nothing came of his victory, at least not immediately.

At the Palm Café, he met Fayne Pridgeon, a beautiful young woman with a penchant for tight skirts and high heels. She was a fixture at the club. It turned out she was Sam Cooke's former girlfriend. She and Hendrix quickly moved in together, and she introduced Hendrix to the club's owners, who occasionally let him sit in with the house band. In the audience one night was Tony Rice, a friend of the Isley Brothers', the famous soul group whose hits included the high-energy standard "Shout." It so happened that the Isleys were looking for a new guitarist for their revue-style show. Bowled over by Hendrix's playing, Rice recommended him to the Isleys. He played for them one afternoon and was hired on the spot. Hendrix played on the group's next single, "Testify," and then in March 1964 went out on tour with them.

The Isleys took Hendrix to places he had never been, north to Montreal and south to Bermuda. They also spotlighted him for a 20-second solo during every set and let him cut loose on stage. Hendrix was inclined to do so anyway, and the crowds ate it up. Although he appreciated the chance to strut his stuff, he chafed at the stylistic constraints of "white mohair suits, patent leather shoes, and patent leather hairdos." Finally, tired of being just one guy on a crowded bandstand, he quit the show when it came to Nashville and briefly rejoined George Odell for another package tour—until he missed the tour bus in Kansas City and became stranded. But luck was with Hendrix, and just a few days later he was hired by a group that took him to Atlanta. Being in Atlanta landed him his next job with one of rock and roll's early heroes: Little Richard, who was mounting a comeback after several years as a touring preacher. Hendrix quit the Little Richard tour in Los Angeles, then rejoined and remained with the tour until it reached New York.

In New York, Hendrix soon joined one of the city's top R&B club groups, Curtis Knight and the Squires. With this gig, Hendrix would enjoy a new level of exposure in the New York City area for the next eight months. He was finally commanding respect from members of the city's rhythm and blues elite.

Egged on by Knight and his fellow Squires, Hendrix took long solos, peeling off beautiful blues passages with his long, strong, graceful fingers, sometimes flipping the guitar up to his face and playing it with his teeth—a stunt that astounded onlookers.

Hendrix also gigged with Joey Dee and the Starlighters of "Peppermint Twist" fame and, on and off, with King Curtis and the Kingpins. Probably his oddest job during that time—in fact, probably the oddest job of his entire career—was as a session player backing up B-movie star Jayne Mansfield (known as the poor man's Marilyn Monroe) in her bid for recording-star status—a bid that failed miserably.

At 22, Hendrix finally had steady work, but the pay was still lousy, and he was back living in New York, either in cheap hotels

With Little Richard

The Jimmy Hendrix–Little Richard connection was a brief and stormy one. Little Richard, a flamboyant performer with an electrifying voice and a temper to match, was not the type to share the spotlight with anybody, especially a member of his backup band. He was the star; they were hired help. Suddenly, however, he had to deal with an upstart guitarist who went onstage in flamboyant clothes and performed flashy guitar tricks for the crowd—Little Richard's crowd. Hendrix's showmanship infuriated the man who was paying his way. "I am Little Richard, and I am the King of Rock 'n' Rhythm and I am the only one who's going to look pretty on stage!" he ranted one night after a show. Once, Hendrix went onstage wearing a frilly ruffled shirt, and Little Richard not only fined him five dollars, he also demanded that he give up the garment. Tired of his boss's tyrannical ways, Hendrix quit the Little Richard tour soon after it hit Los Angeles.

In Los Angeles, Hendrix met and romanced a young backup singer named Rosa Lee Brooks, who hooked him up with Ike and Tina Turner. He played a few shows with the Ike and Tina Turner Revue, but he soon bit the bullet and rejoined Little Richard. He said good-bye to Brooks and stayed with the tour until it reached New York, where—depending on whose version is the truth—Hendrix was either fired by Little Richard's brother/road manager, or he quit.

or crashing in friends' apartments. "I still have my guitar and amp and as long as I have that, no fool can keep me from living," he wrote to his father in a letter dated August 8, 1965. "It could be worse than this, but I'm going to keep hustling and scuffling until I get things happening like they're supposed to for me."

What he wanted, more than anything, was to play and sing his own songs. He knew he had the guitar craft. He also had a head full of ideas. He was not so sure about his voice—particularly after working behind gifted vocalists like Sam Cooke, Little Richard, and Curtis Knight—but he knew that outside the rhythm-and-blues milieu, a singer did not have to have a rich, gospel-tutored set of pipes to sound right for a particular song. Case in point was a young singer/songwriter from the Midwest named Bob Dylan.

Dylan had been on the folk scene for several years, but starting with his stunning performance at the Newport Folk Festival in Newport, Rhode Island, in July 1965, Dylan became a trailblazer in the "electric folk" movement. It was popular mostly with white kids in the cities and suburbs—not the sort of music anyone would play in Harlem. Hendrix started to hang around the coffeehouses down in Greenwich Village to hear groups that were experimenting with rock, folk, blues, beat poetry, and a new sound soon categorized as folk rock. Dylan's latest album, *Highway 61 Revisited*, with its sparse vocals, poetic lyrics, and freewheeling melodies, piqued Hendrix's interest in the new direction that rock and roll was taking. Dylan's voice—more a half-spoken nasal rasp that conveyed the meaning of the words as much as the words themselves—also convinced Hendrix that he, too, could sing if he wanted to.

It was another musician, Richie Havens—a folk singer starting to make a name for himself in the Village—who finally persuaded Hendrix to blaze his own trail, too. Havens caught Hendrix performing at the midtown Cheetah dance club as part of King Curtis's band and prodded him to leave Harlem (where, in fact, Hendrix never felt his wild style really fit in) and investigate the

This photograph shows Jimmy Hendrix in the early 1960s. After playing as a backup guitarist for the Isley Brothers, Little Richard, and Curtis Knight and the Squires, Hendrix realized his greatest desire was to play and sing his own songs. He began to perform on his own, playing at small clubs, like Café Wha?, in Greenwich Village.

Village scene. He told Hendrix it was time to strike out on his own, not just be a backup player for other musicians. Hendrix took the advice. He grew out his hair to the now-iconic untamed Afro and felt comfortable in the bohemian, artistic environment. He began turning up at open auditions and getting booked into small clubs, like the Night Owl Café and Café Wha?

JIMI IS BORN

Around this time, a girlfriend bought Hendrix his first Fender Stratocaster guitar, and he spent hours filing down the frets so he could restring it left-handed. Hendrix's love of Strats was an affair that would last the rest of his life. The Strat's easy action and narrow neck were perfect for Hendrix's evolving style and enhanced his amazing dexterity: His hands were so large and his fingers so long that he could fret across all six strings with the top joint of his thumb alone, plus he could play lead and rhythm parts simultaneously. Also at this time, "Jimmy Hendrix" ceased to be, for in the summer of 1966, he renamed himself Jimi James. And it would be as "Jimi" that he would be forever remembered.

Jimi formed his own band, the Blue Flames, which included Randy Wolfe on rhythm guitar, Danny Casey on drums, and Randy Palmer on bass. To distinguish the two Randys from each other, Hendrix dubbed Wolfe "Randy California" (a name that would stick throughout his professional life) for his home state, and Palmer became "Randy Texas." Wolfe was a gifted teenage player whom Hendrix had met at a music store in Midtown Manhattan the night of Hendrix's first gig at Café Wha? Wolfe impressed him with his slide guitar talent. Hendrix shopped the new band around to Village club owners. It was like starting from scratch—he was reaching for a different audience now. He was also back to being broke.

Having given up his steady gigs, Hendrix resorted to looking to friends for help. He crashed in lofts with other musicians, some of whom, like David Crosby and Roger McGuinn, would go on to their own fame. Word of Hendrix's guitar prowess spread quickly through the downtown grapevine, and he had some of the city's best young musicians coming to hear him or to play alongside him as best they could. Fluid in seemingly any style, Hendrix simply blew away most of his peers. The admiration, however, did not clothe or feed him. Plus, his beloved Stratocaster was stolen just a couple of weeks after he got it.

Blues musician John Hammond, Jr., later recalled:

> When I first met Jimi, he was destitute. I was playing at a club called the Gaslight. Across the street was the Café Wha?, a really funky joint. Jimi was playing there, and I went by one night. He was playing some of my songs.... He was incredible-looking and seemed pleased to meet me. I asked him how I could help, and he said: 'Get me a gig. Get me out of here!' So I got him a gig at the Café Au Go Go, and I worked there with him for a month with Jimi playing lead guitar.

Hendrix's reputation attracted a number of famous musicians, including the Beatles (who had come to America to tour and were playing at Shea Stadium at the time), Paul Butterfield and Michael Bloomfield of the Butterfield Blues Band, and Hendrix's idol, Bob Dylan. Bloomfield later commented on how Hendrix was able to get sounds and notes out of his Stratocaster that completely mystified him. "How he did this, I wish I understood," he recalled some years later in an interview in *Guitar Player*. After seeing Hendrix in action, "I didn't even want to pick up a guitar for the next year."

In the audience at one of Hendrix's gigs was a young woman from England, the girlfriend of Rolling Stones guitarist Keith Richards, who was on tour at the time. When Hendrix's set ended, she invited him back to her hotel. There they talked for hours about music—they shared a love of the blues—and there Hendrix took LSD for the first time. Linda Keith became Hendrix's champion, promoting him whenever she could to whomever she thought would help him make it big. After striking out a few times—Hendrix left the Stones' manager and a record company owner unimpressed—she finally scored in early August 1966 with a musician acquaintance. Chas Chandler, the bass player for the British group the Animals, was in New York, playing on his final American tour. He was looking to become a manager when the tour ended. At Linda Keith's urging, he dropped in at Café Wha? and saw Hendrix perform.

Once was all it took. Chandler could hardly believe that this remarkable guitarist had not been signed by a record label or management company. He approached Hendrix and said, "I believe you'll be a sensation in Britain." Hendrix asked if Chandler knew Eric Clapton, the revered British electric-blues guitarist. Chandler said he did and promised an introduction if Hendrix came to England. The two huddled in the basement bar for a long time, hammering out the basics of a deal that would bring Hendrix to London, where he would assemble a band to record and play his own songs. Chandler and Michael Jeffery, the Animals' manager in England, would be partners in managing his career.

Over the next month and a half, while Chandler finished his tour with the Animals, the ball was set in motion to settle everything and to get a copy of Hendrix's birth certificate from Seattle so that he could get a passport. Hendrix continued to perform at the Café Wha? with the Blue Flames. Finally, on September 23, 1966, with $40 borrowed from a musician friend in his pocket, his guitar, and a change of clothes packed into the guitar case, Jimi Hendrix boarded a plane at Kennedy Airport bound for London. The bird's-eye view of New York City stretched out below the soaring plane would be Hendrix's last glimpse of America for nearly a year.

4

Fire

Chas Chandler spent the entire flight plotting Jimi Hendrix's launch onto the British music scene—equipment, money, clothes, auditions, a band, studio time, tour dates, press, publicity. A thornier problem faced Hendrix, however, when he stepped off the plane at Heathrow International Airport at 9 A.M. on Saturday, September 24, 1966: British immigration officers. They put Hendrix through the mill. He did not have a work permit, so Chandler came up with the ruse that Hendrix was a songwriter who had come to collect royalties owed to him. The authorities believed the story, and Hendrix was issued a seven-day visa.

From the airport, Chandler went immediately to the home of a musician named Zoot Money, whose house was a meeting place for other musicians. Money and his wife, Ronnie, also had several musicians rooming in their house. One of them was Andy Summers, who went on to join the Police.

Another boarder was a beautiful 20-year-old part-time DJ named Kathy Etchingham, who knew many of the top musicians in the business, including the Rolling Stones and the Who. Introductions were made, and Hendrix picked up a guitar and started jamming with Money and Summers. That night, he also sat in with some local musicians at a club called the Scotch of St. James, giving London club crawlers—including Etchingham—a preview of what was to come. The crowd was stunned. They had never seen or heard anyone like Jimi Hendrix. Etchingham and Hendrix spent time together at the club, and she immediately became his new girlfriend—as well as his entrée into the music scene. The future looked bright.

JAMMING WITH CLAPTON

It became even brighter when, within days, Chandler kept his promise and introduced Hendrix to Eric Clapton, who had just formed his new band, Cream. On October 1, Hendrix had the chance to jam with the guitar legend. Clapton was blown away—and not a little uneasy: The king's throne was being usurped by a nobody newcomer. Word quickly spread about the guitar duel, and the young lions of rock, many of whom had conquered America during the first wave of the British Invasion, were coming to see this American in their midst. Pete Townshend of the Who, Mick Jagger of the Rolling Stones, Paul McCartney of the Beatles, and Jeff Beck of the Yardbirds all checked out the phenomenal young guitarist who played rock and absolutely authentic blues. They marveled at his unbelievable playing and expressive, aggressive showmanship on stage.

In an interview in the December 14, 1995, issue of *Rolling Stone,* Mick Jagger recollected:

> I loved Jimi Hendrix from the beginning. The moment
> I saw him, I thought he was fantastic. I was an instant
> convert.... He didn't have a very good voice but made

Swingin' London of the 1960s was epitomized by the Carnaby Street fashion scene, shown here, and British rock bands. The young Brits' "mod" scene was quite different from the hippie movement taking place in the United States.

up for it with his guitar. I first saw him at the Revolution Club in London. I was one of six people in the club, and Jimi was playing. I couldn't believe it. It was insane—so good, and the whole idea of this kind of English band behind him, this bizarre mixture between a blues performer and a rock player with an English touch.

London in 1966 was the epicenter of cultural cool, thanks to British rock bands and the Carnaby Street fashion scene, spearheaded a couple of years earlier by designer Mary Quant and hairdresser Vidal Sassoon. The young Brits who belonged to the city's "mod" scene, shown so vividly in the

1966 film *Blowup*, flaunted their cool and were aloof to anything that happened before dusk. London's "youthquake" bore only a faint resemblance to the spirited hippie culture blooming across the Atlantic in the United States.

Chas Chandler put out the word to the scene makers of London that he had brought home an amazing young guitarist from the United States who would, he promised, astonish and electrify. The British delighted in boosting American artists who were underappreciated or overlooked in their own country, including such blues masters as Muddy Waters and Mississippi John Hurt. The fact that Hendrix, too, was black only added to his credibility, as far as Londoners were concerned. Chandler saw Hendrix doing more than just following in that tradition. He would cause a sensation. He would blow people's minds. First, though, he needed a band.

FORMING THE EXPERIENCE

Chandler and Hendrix decided to keep the lineup lean; only a bassist and a drummer would fill out the band. Hendrix could sing well enough for rock and roll, and, more important, he could generate more sound with his Fender Stratocaster than most bands with two guitarists.

Guitarist Noel Redding walked in on the first day of auditions. He had played in a handful of British bands—none of which, he concluded, was going anywhere. He had actually come to audition for a slot in the New Animals, but Chandler asked if he would be interested in joining Hendrix's band instead—if he could play bass. He could not, but he gave it a try and jammed with Hendrix on a few songs. He was surprisingly good. Redding intrigued Hendrix even before he played a note. Redding was lean-faced and handsome with a frizzy red Afro and wire-rimmed glasses that perched on the end of his aristocratic nose. He looked British, yet somehow exotic. "I dug his hairstyle," Hendrix later said, "so I asked him to play bass."

Redding agreed to the switch. Besides, as he later said, "I [couldn't] see anybody else playing lead guitar with this bloke." He was hired right away. Hendrix's band was two-thirds complete. All it needed was a drummer.

Mitch Mitchell believed the gig was his if he wanted it. A short, wiry Briton with boyish looks, he knew his way around a drum kit and had spent much of his life in front of audiences, first as a child actor and then as a drummer in a series of British pop and swing bands. The last of these was called, coincidentally, Georgie Fame and the Blue Flames, which had played a few gigs with the Animals. Mitchell, only 19 years old, was between bands when Chandler called and encouraged him to stop by. Game for anything, Mitchell was a cocky little sprite who impressed Hendrix and Chandler with his musical and rhythmic dexterity. He got the job.

Neither Mitchell nor Redding knew quite what to make of the guitarist they were chosen to accompany. Except for the blues musicians who toured Great Britain, neither lad had had much contact with black Americans. Hendrix was an enigma, wild looking but quiet, low-key in his treatment of other people but uninhibited, even crazy, with his guitar.

In his book, *Jimi Hendrix: Inside the Experience*, Mitchell wrote:

> At the audition, it was strange. I met this black guy with very, very wild hair wearing this Burberry raincoat. He looked very straight, really, apart from the hair. We didn't talk much at first.... [Jimi] was very soft-spoken and gave the impression of being very gentle, almost shy. It was immediately apparent that he was a good guitarist; but at that stage I was more knocked out that he could cover so many different styles, as well. You name it, he could do it. I think we did 'Have Mercy Babe' first. [Jimi] didn't really sing, more mumbled along to the music—Chas really had to coax it out of him.

Next, the band needed a name. As Redding remembered it, it was Mike Jeffery, Chandler's business partner, who came up with "The Jimi Hendrix Experience"—reasoning that the band *was* an experience. One of Hendrix's recent public jam sessions had attracted Johnny Hallyday, considered the French Elvis by his countrymen. He invited Hendrix and his band to tour with him for two weeks in France. Fortunately, Chandler and Jeffery had quietly worked out Hendrix's visa problems, so they were ready to go.

THE DEBUT

The Jimi Hendrix Experience played its first gig on October 13, 1966, at a concert hall called Novelty in Evreux, France. The trio played a 15-minute set of cover songs that included "Hey Joe" and "Killin' Floor," revved up by Hendrix's incendiary licks, Redding's brisk bass lines, and Mitchell's agile drumming, which Hendrix particularly enjoyed. Mitchell treated music like a competitive sport; he seemed to relish pushing Hendrix, daring him to match or surpass his own fireworks if he could. The tour ended with a sold-out show at the 2,500-seat L'Olympia in Paris.

Despite the good crowds, reviews of the first Experience dates in France were dismissive. "Bad mixture of James Brown and Chuck Berry," one critic wrote after the Evreux show. Indeed, the band was rough, having barely played together. In Paris several days later, however, the story was completely different. The band was much more in sync, and the audience went wild over Hendrix.

Chandler, though, had more than a good show on his mind. The band needed a single. Without a record, there would be no next level for the Jimi Hendrix Experience, much less a return on the manager's already considerable investment. He had pawned five of his six guitars to pay for equipment and tour costs. He wanted that single out quickly. On October 23—a week after returning from France—the band went into the recording studio and laid down the tracks for "Hey Joe." Chandler also wanted Hendrix to write a song of his own. Though reluctant to think of himself as a songwriter, Hendrix managed to write a song in one night. He called it "Stone Free."

The band soon was booked into a club in Munich, Germany, a four-night, two-shows-a-night gig. The crowds grew bigger with each show, and Hendrix's German fans got more of an "experience" than had been planned. One night, Hendrix accidentally cracked the neck on his guitar. In a 1968 interview in the weekly British music magazine *New Musical Express* (better known as *NME*), Chandler recalled, "When he picked it up, he saw that it had cracked.... He just went barmy and smashed everything in sight. The German audience loved it, and we decided to keep it as part of the act when there was good press."

The single was scheduled to be released on December 16, 1966. To promote "Hey Joe," the band debuted the song that same day on the British television program *Ready, Steady, Go!* The single hit the record stores and, slowly at first, began to sell and find its way onto the radio.

EXPOSURE

The Experience also caught the eye of the British press. The first write-ups were sometimes mocking and occasionally racist. WILD MAN OF BORNEO read a headline in the British publication *Disc and Music Echo*. But Chas Chandler relished such reactions: The more the press gasped at this "wild man" with the kinky hair and noisy guitar, the more British youths would tune in and listen. Hendrix certainly had his journalistic admirers, too. Keith Altham reported in *NME*: "Hendrix is a one-man guitar explosion with a stage act which leaves those who think pop has gone pretty with their mouths hanging open. What this man does to a guitar could get him arrested for assault."

A club date at the hip London venue Bag O' Nails earned Hendrix his first interview, a November 1966 article titled

"Mr. Phenomenon!" for the *Record Mirror.* In it, he told the interviewer that he did not like to pigeonhole his sound. "I'd like it to be called 'Free Feeling.' It's a mixture of rock, freak-out, blues, and rave music." Sometimes the press had a slightly different take on Hendrix. With Britain's rock aristocracy and the press giving Hendrix their seal of approval, the record-company executives, radio people, and tour promoters were taking notice.

Aside from having a unique sound, Hendrix also had a unique look. Based on his taste for Old-World finery, he would go onstage in a gold-braided nineteenth-century cavalry jacket or stride about London like some psychedelic Mozart in embroidered velvet jackets, crushed-velvet pants, ruffled shirts, and dark glasses. He also began acquiring a steady taste for alcohol and drugs, especially speed and hashish.

The Experience's early live shows thrived on disarray and on the band's ability to skirt a collapse in midflight, with Hendrix somehow simultaneously holding it all together and pushing the music outward into places nobody had gone before. He brandished his guitar like a torch, slicing fresh contours into a sonic wall. The sound moved and flowed to currents directed by Hendrix's hands, twisting into shapes that split, subdivided, merged, and then reconfigured—like echoes—into something familiar but always new.

On January 11, 1967, the band was in the recording studio all day, laying down tracks for its first album on Track Records, which was being bankrolled by Polydor. (The contract the band signed with its managers decidedly favored Chandler and Jeffery financially. Occasionally one or more of the band members would complain about their financial arrangement, but Chandler and Jeffery usually smoothed over the problem by handing over some cash.) Hendrix had written one of the songs a few weeks before in his dressing room during a concert intermission; it would become his signature song: "Purple Haze." Originally a 20-minute composition, the song had to be cut drastically for commercial reasons.

That same night after leaving the studio, the band performed at the Bag O' Nails. The crowd was "the ultimate who's who of London's rock elite," as Charles Cross put it in *Room Full of Mirrors*. "If the proverbial bomb had been dropped on the Bag that evening, the British music scene might have ceased to exist." Among those in the audience were three of the four Beatles—Paul McCartney, John Lennon, and Ringo Starr—and their manager, Brian Epstein; Mick Jagger and Brian Jones of the Rolling Stones; Pete Townshend; Donovan; the members of Small Faces and the Animals; and guitar wizards Eric Clapton, Jeff Beck, and Jimmy Page. Cross tells how singer Terry Reid "went to the bathroom at one point and, coming back, bumped into Brian Jones. 'It's all wet down in the front,' Jones warned. Reid replied: 'What are

The Myth of "Purple Haze"

It is common knowledge that what is perhaps Jimi Hendrix's best-known song—with perhaps his best-known lyric, "'Scuse me while I kiss the sky"—is about a psychedelic experience as a result of taking LSD. Or is it? Written in 1966 in a dressing room of the club he was performing in, "Purple Haze" was originally much longer than the recorded version, and Hendrix felt that the original concept of the song was lost when it was shortened. According to a 1967 interview, he said that the song was actually about traveling through a mythical land and was inspired by his love of science fiction. Another time, he said that it was about a dream he had of "walking under the sea." At other times, however, he implied that it was inspired by a Hopi legend, while another time he said that the song was about being so hung up on a girl "that he's in, ya know, a sort of daze.... That's what the song is all about." Every time he was asked what "Purple Haze" was actually about, he gave a different answer. Adding to the mystery, the title on his original draft was "Purple Haze—Jesus Saves." In any event, it isn't likely that we will ever really know what inspired the song—but sometimes a little mystery isn't a bad thing.

you talking about? I can't see any water.' To which Jones said, 'It's wet from all the guitar players crying.' " (Also in the audience was Roger Mayer, an electronics whiz then working for the Royal Navy Scientific Service, whose hobby was creating effects devices, like fuzz-tone boxes, for guitars. He soon made them exclusively for Hendrix.)

U.S. RECORD DEAL

Meanwhile, Mike Jeffery went to the United States and, touting the success of "Hey Joe," returned to Britain in March, having pulled off a coup: a deal with Warner Brothers Records for the U.S. release of *Are You Experienced* for a $150,000 advance—an unheard-of amount of money for an unknown band. Jeffery was nothing if not persuasive—even though, Chandler suspected, he was probably robbing the band and hiding most of the income in offshore accounts.

"Hey Joe" peaked at number four on the British charts in February. Before their album's release, the Experience joined a monthlong two-shows-a-night tour around England. Headlined by the Walker Brothers, the show also featured Cat Stevens and tuxedoed balladeer Engelbert Humperdinck. The Jimi Hendrix Experience would be the opening act. Chandler and Hendrix were determined to make the band stand out on opening night. They spent hours working out stage routines, body language, the timing of song introductions, even the suggestive way Hendrix stroked the neck and body of his guitar. Now they wanted to raise the theatrical pitch another notch. When smashing his guitar was nixed as being Pete Townshend's trick, someone joked that it was too bad that he could not set his guitar on fire. It was an idea that Hendrix would run with.

The Finsbury Park Astoria concert hall in London was jammed with eager spectators on March 31, 1967, as the Experience galloped through a brisk set. When the band finished "Fire," a new song, Hendrix tossed his Fender

The Jimi Hendrix Experience included (from left) Noel Redding, Hendrix, and Mitch Mitchell. The band quickly became popular in Great Britain and the rest of Europe. To really make it big, though, Hendrix's management knew he would have to make an impact in the United States.

Stratocaster to the floor of the stage, dropped to his knees, doused the guitar with the flammable liquid, and tried to light it. Nothing happened. He tried again. And again. On the fourth try, his guitar went up in flames. As Hendrix waved the burning instrument around, the Finsbury Park audience went berserk.

Not so pleased by Hendrix's stunt were the theater manager and a city fire marshal standing backstage. The other acts were also angry at being upstaged. There was talk of dropping the Experience from the tour. British newspapers were complaining about Hendrix's stage demeanor. "His movements were far too suggestive for an audience mostly in the 14–18 age group," the *Lincolnshire Chronicle* fretted. But the tour promoters also knew that controversy boosted receipts at the box office. Jimi Hendrix was a smash. He was who people were coming to see.

The band finished recording its album on April 4, 1967. In May, the Jimi Hendrix Experience released another single, a dreamy, spartan ballad called "The Wind Cries Mary." Hendrix wrote it after a heated argument with his live-in girlfriend, Kathy Etchingham (her middle name is Mary). When *Are You Experienced* was released later that month, the 11-song tour through Hendrix's musical psyche veered from baroque ("Manic Depression") to blues ("Red House"), its stylistic wanderings always yanked back to earth by the ferocity of the guitar, bass, and drums.

The album shot to number three in Great Britain, two notches below the top spot occupied by the Beatles' *Sgt. Pepper's Lonely Hearts Club Band*. The British could not get enough of Jimi Hendrix. Crowds crammed concert halls (which tour promoters deliberately overbooked) to watch him play, writhe, smash his guitar through his amplifier, and walk offstage with his shattered equipment still screeching through loudspeakers. Hendrix began to find the response disconcerting. He enjoyed theatrics; they could be as expressive as his guitar work. But he also had begun to notice that he could step onstage and play well or play badly, and nobody seemed to notice either way. Whatever he served, the crowds would eat it up. They just wanted Hendrix to live up to his hype.

The Experience conquered England and Europe in short order, and the speed of their ascent convinced Chas Chandler and Mike Jeffery that bigger things were coming. Even with the Jimi Hendrix Experience topping British charts, the band was still making very little money playing live. For Hendrix to truly establish himself as an artist and a star, he had to make it big at home, and that was exactly what the band did at Monterey.

5

The Experience

The opportunity for the Jimi Hendrix Experience to make a major splash in the United States came as a result of a happy accident of timing. San Francisco and Los Angeles were the spawning grounds for an emerging music scene, and Chas Chandler and Mike Jeffery had already lined up dates at the Fillmore in San Francisco—run by the dynamic rock impresario Bill Graham—when John Philips (of the Mamas and the Papas) and producer Lou Adler got the idea for the Monterey International Pop Festival. The fact that Paul McCartney was on the festival's board and was an ardent supporter of Hendrix and his band was yet another lucky fluke.

When Jimi Hendrix played that final night at the festival, his image was burned into the minds of all those at Monterey. Reviewers were divided. "When Jimi left the stage, he graduated from rumor to legend," said one, although another called the performance "a vulgar parody of rock theatrics." Virtually every review, though, called the Jimi Hendrix Experience the most unforgettable act of the concert—and as the old expression goes, there is no such thing as bad publicity.

Hendrix's fame had burst open. Not just the crowd but the musicians backstage had been blown away by his performance. "You killed them, man!" South African jazz great Hugh Masekela had crowed. "You killed them!" echoed a beaming Brian Jones, who had come from England just to see Hendrix play.

Word of Hendrix's triumph at Monterey had traveled over the West Coast grapevine: Jimi Hendrix took rock and roll, expanded it through his musical virtuosity, added electronics and showbiz pizzazz, and dressed it in flamboyant finery to create a whole new sound. As the concept applied to his music—and to much of his life, for that matter—there were no limits. In San Francisco, crowds jammed the Fillmore for the band's entire six-day run. Graham was so pleased that he gave the Experience a $2,000 bonus and presented each band member with an engraved antique watch. Soon after, Peter Tork of the Monkees invited Jimi Hendrix to his Laurel Canyon mansion to party with the likes of David Crosby, Judy Collins, Joni Mitchell, Mama Cass Elliot, and Mike Bloomfield. Hendrix also went to Stephen Stills's house in Malibu for a jam—fueled by LSD—that lasted nearly an entire day.

A DUBIOUS TOUR

Mike Jeffery, meanwhile, had run off to New York. It was rapidly becoming his trademark to disappear and then, like a diver snorkeling for loot in a sunken galley, resurface with some breathtaking prize. Sure enough, when he called Chandler, Jeffery had big news: He had landed the band a spot as a supporting act on a nationwide tour with the teen-idol band the Monkees—or the Prefab Four, as critics called Micky Dolenz, Peter Tork, Davy Jones, and Mike Nesmith, whose group had been created solely as a TV version of the Beatles. Teaming the Jimi Hendrix Experience with the Monkees would be one

Soon after its pyrotechnic triumph at the Monterey International Pop Festival, the Jimi Hendrix Experience was contracted to tour with the Monkees, a made-for-TV band that was a favorite with preteens. The match only lasted five concerts. Here, the Monkees pose in a promotional portrait. They are (clockwise from rear left) Michael Nesmith, Davy Jones, Peter Tork, and Micky Dolenz.

of the strangest pairings in show business history, and one that—unsurprisingly—did not last long.

Chandler was aghast. "Are you out of your ... mind?!" he screamed into the phone. It was incomprehensible: His business partner had just contracted the flamboyant, sexually provocative Jimi Hendrix to open for a band whose core audience was barely out of footed pajamas. Chandler suddenly saw all he had worked for crashing into a laughable heap. Hendrix on a bill with the Monkees would become a joke.

Jeffery saw the situation differently. Here was a chance for exposure, he reasoned; the Monkees were the most popular band in the country next to the Beatles. And because they wanted to be taken seriously by the rock community as well as develop a fan base beyond pre-teens, the Monkees eagerly agreed to bring Hendrix aboard. In fact, Dolenz and Tork had come up with the idea, having seen the band play at Monterey and believing that the theatricality of both groups would mesh. Chandler, though, was certain that the tour would be a disaster and flew to New York to tell his partner he would have no part of it. Hendrix was as furious as Chandler. He loathed the Monkees—in an interview with *Melody Maker* magazine a few months earlier, he said, "Oh, God, I hate them! Dishwater. I really hate somebody like that to make it so big. You can't knock anybody for making it, but people like the Monkees?!" But the papers were signed. The Experience could not back out now.

After the Fillmore shows, the Experience performed in Santa Barbara. The band then played its first Los Angeles gig, at the Whisky A Go Go. This appearance, too, drew a crowd of rock's elite, including Mama Cass Elliot and Jim Morrison of the Doors. From there, the band flew to New York for a couple of engagements at small clubs and then down to Jacksonville, Florida, for the start of the Monkees tour. The choice of opening city could not have been worse. The South was still very racist, very segregated, in 1967, and here were thousands of lily-white teenyboppers waiting for their adorable heroes.

Instead they got, as Micky Dolenz described it in his book, *I'm A Believer*, "this black guy in a psychedelic DayGlo blouse, playing music from hell, … then lighting [his guitar] on fire." Not exactly what the audience was expecting to see or hear.

The Experience was slated to play 25-minute sets—warm-up routines, basically—with the house lights still up and youngsters still filing into their seats, parents in tow. A sullen Jimi Hendrix would greet the crowd with an attention-getting blast from his guitar, volume cranked, the signal going off like an air raid in his listeners' little ears. A few youngsters seemed to get a charge from the mayhem, but others were frightened. Parents who had brought their children to hear "Pleasant Valley Sunday" and other Monkees ditties were aghast. Only the Monkees themselves appreciated and understood Hendrix's music, especially Tork, who thought Hendrix's virtuosity was "exquisite." Aside from the Monkees' endless stash of hash, though, Hendrix thought the tour was a waste of time.

The debacle lasted for all of five engagements. Even Mike Jeffery could see that he had made a mistake. Chandler approached tour promoter Dick Clark—best-known as the host of the wildly popular squeaky-clean teen dance show *American Bandstand*—and persuaded him that Hendrix and the Monkees were a disastrous combination. But they both agreed that the Monkees would look foolish if their opening act bailed on them; some sort of cover story was needed. The Hendrix camp came up with an idea and issued a phony press release saying the Experience was being dropped because the Daughters of the American Revolution (DAR), an influential (and conservative) women's organization, found Hendrix's theatrics vulgar, outrageous, and "too erotic," plainly unsuitable for children. The story sounded plausible; indeed, the thought of Hendrix scandalizing a group of prim, elderly white ladies with his oversexed stage act was too wickedly delightful to resist. None of the publications that ran the press release even bothered to call the DAR for confirmation.

The members of the Experience—(from left) Noel Redding, Jimi Hendrix, and Mitch Mitchell—arrived at Heathrow International Airport on August 21, 1967. After their disastrous tour with the Monkees, Jimi Hendrix and the band played several successful gigs at the Café Au Go Go in Greenwich Village and opened for the Mamas and Papas at the Hollywood Bowl.

Hendrix played the last of the Monkees dates on July 16, 1967, at Forest Hills Stadium in Queens, New York, ending one of the daffiest partnerships in rock and roll history. Laughing about the poor fit, Hendrix told the *New Musical Express*: "I think they're replacing me with Mickey Mouse."

BACK IN THE VILLAGE

Left with a large hole in its schedule, the band did some more recording and played a few dates in New York—including a triumphant engagement at the Café Au Go Go, where Hendrix had last played as Jimi James. For a month, the Experience played various clubs in Greenwich Village—jamming with musicians like Bob Dylan, Curtis Knight, John Hammond, Jr., Ted Nugent, Al Kooper, and Roger McGuinn. The band also played several shows at the Ambassador Theater in Washington, D.C., and a club in Ann Arbor, Michigan. Then the Experience returned to California to open for the Mamas and the Papas at the Hollywood Bowl. They flew back to England on August 21, 1967.

Warner Brothers finally released the U.S. version of *Are You Experienced?* (the American release bore a question mark in the title) on September 1. It would include three songs omitted from the European version ("Purple Haze," "Hey Joe," and "The Wind Cries Mary"). Warner executives were dubious about the album's prospects—despite the generally favorable reviews—but they had invested in Hendrix and felt obliged to try. *Are You Experienced?* entered *Billboard*'s Top 200 chart at 190. The album would spend the next 106 weeks on the chart, peaking at number five. Jimi Hendrix was now a certified rock star.

6

Purple Haze

The group spent the rest of 1967 in Europe. It toured, played for radio and television, and recorded tracks for a second album. *Axis: Bold as Love* was released in England on December 1, 1967—four days after Jimi's twenty-fifth birthday. In contrast to the nonstop rocket ride of *Are You Experienced*, *Axis* was filled with dreamy, metaphysical blues steeped in Native American mythology and drenched in lush noise conjured by Hendrix and his studio collaborator, an inventive young engineer from South Africa named Eddie Kramer. Colors bled beautifully through waterfall ballads like "Little Wing" and "Castles Made of Sand." Hendrix also blended multiple instruments—harpsichord, flute, and glockenspiel—with special effects and backward-recorded guitar to create a sensory bath in full stereo. Even the soaring level of creativity of the tracks on *Axis* set Jimi Hendrix apart. He simply sounded like nobody else.

The reviews were uniformly ecstatic. Critics lauded the cohesive blend of hard rock, jazz, and R&B. The recording sessions themselves, though, had started to show the cracks in the cohesion of the band. Redding recorded a vocal track—"She's So Fine"—that Hendrix would not release as a single. He even cut some of Redding's bass lines and rerecorded them himself. No doubt it was done to improve the sound, but it still stung.

Although Hendrix used the metaphor of falling in love to explain the album's title, he still held himself at arm's length from virtually everyone. He continued to share a flat with his girlfriend, Kathy Etchingham, but he was incapable of fidelity, and though he had friends and a community of musicians to whom he truly belonged, he gave more of himself onstage than he did privately. "I don't think anybody knew him," road manager Gerry Stickells later recalled. His early childhood experiences of never knowing emotional security remained firmly in charge of Jimi Hendrix the adult.

The Jimi Hendrix Experience topped the bill everywhere it went. But as splendidly as things were going, something familiar was stealing over Hendrix, a sensation he knew too well. His old restlessness began to surface again. Touring was beginning to feel like a drag, a necessity that got in the way of

IN HIS OWN WORDS...

Unlike with "Purple Haze," Jimi Hendrix had a simple—and single—explanation for the title of the band's second album, *Axis: Bold as Love.* As quoted in *Black Gold*, he told a Swedish radio interviewer on January 8, 1968:

The axis of the Earth, if it changes, it changes the whole face of the Earth like every few thousand years. And it's like love in a human being; if he really falls in love, deep enough, it'll change him. It might change his whole life so both of them can really go together.

songwriting and recording. Even the recording studio could be frustrating because there was never enough time to get the sounds just right; the tour bus was always idling outside, waiting for him to get aboard. On the road, the crowds began to look the same, no matter their enthusiasm. Hendrix sometimes forgot what city he was in, which was not surprising: In 1967, the Experience played 255 shows.

"I'd like to take a six-month break," Hendrix told *Melody Maker* magazine in an interview published on December 23. "I'm tired of trying to write stuff and finding I can't." Good things were still happening, certainly. The band was sharp. Crowds showered Hendrix with affection, and he rewarded them with his inspired playing. Below the surface, though, there was turmoil.

THE CENTER OF HIS UNIVERSE

With album sales and demand for Hendrix's talents climbing, increasing responsibility rode on his shoulders. Hendrix was the franchise. Everything—music, records, tours, profits, the livelihoods of the band and crew—depended on what happened when he picked up a guitar. Everyone orbited around him. Astronomy and the heavens—which fascinated him and which he plumbed even more deeply on the new album—provided an apt metaphor for his personal circumstances. In his universe, he was the sun, the axis, the center of a ring of satellites that needed him for light and warmth; without his creative fires, everything would die out.

It seems likely that Hendrix began to feel the pressure of his situation. On January 3, 1968, in Göteborg, Sweden, after getting drunk, he destroyed his hotel room—every stick of furniture, every curtain, every bit of bed linens; all that remained intact was the phone. He also smashed his right hand through a window. Jimi Hendrix was charged with destruction of property and disturbing the peace, and he spent the night in jail. Fines, legal fees, and hotel reimbursement wiped out more

Jimi Hendrix relaxes on a sofa in this photograph from 1967. He did
not get much rest that year, as the Jimi Hendrix Experience played 255
shows in 1967. The pace continued the following year, as well, with the
Experience playing at larger and larger arenas.

than a third of the band's income from the Swedish dates. The tour was also notable to Hendrix for a far different reason: He would meet Eva Sundqvist, a young university student. When Hendrix next visited Sweden, Sundqvist would become pregnant with his son.

The Experience finished its second European tour at L'Olympia in Paris, where the group had opened for Johnny Hallyday 15 months earlier. Venues that once booked the Experience as a warm-up act were now trumpeting the band with posters and playbills done up in a riot of psychedelic colors. Gigs that had brought minimal fees a year earlier were now bringing in thousands of dollars.

On January 10, 1968, *Axis: Bold as Love*, already flying off the shelves in Great Britain, appeared in U.S. record stores and eventually climbed to number three in the course of a 53-week stay on the charts. The band's first headlining U.S. tour was planned to coincide with the American release of *Axis*: a grueling 49 cities in 51 days, plus whatever last-minute bookings might be thrown in. The tour started in San Francisco, with shows again at the Fillmore—now called the Fillmore West with the opening of the Fillmore East in New York's East Village—as well as at the Winterland. Gigs followed in Arizona and back in California. From there the band would head north to Hendrix's hometown. He was facing the prospect of a return home with some trepidation: He had not been back to Seattle since 1961, and he had been out of touch with his family of late. Hendrix did know, though, that in 1966 his father had remarried, to a Japanese woman named Ayako Fujita Jinka, who called herself "June." June had five children, the youngest of whom, Janie—the only one still living at home—Al Hendrix had adopted.

A FAMILY REUNION

When Hendrix learned that the tour would be taking him to Seattle, he called his father to tell him. Al and Leon Hendrix were at the airport to greet him, along with his new stepmother and stepsister. Hendrix returned to Al's house with his family, where more family members, old family friends, and neighbors stopped in to say hello.

That night Hendrix played at the Seattle Center Arena with his entire family smiling up at him from the front row. His usual erotic performance was a no-show that night; instead, Hendrix played the concert "absolutely straight"—no doubt in deference to his family, wanting to please his father and make a good impression on his stepmother. After the show, he returned to his father's house, where he stayed up all night playing games and drinking with his brother Leon. To Jimi's disappointment, Leon had become a street hustler without much of a future. In *Room Full of Mirrors*, Charles R. Cross wrote, "[Jimi] told his brother to straighten out, but his exhortations would have little effect: Jimi knew that Leon's childhood had been as difficult as his own, and there had not been the saving grace of the guitar for Leon. Though Leon displayed artistic skill ... [he] was constantly compared to his older, more talented sibling."

Jimi Hendrix had arranged for a special free concert early the next morning at his old school, Garfield High. Hungover and exhausted, Hendrix arrived at his alma mater to discover that his bandmates were nowhere to be found. Nor was there an instrument for him to play. Hendrix shuffled awkwardly behind a microphone in the school gym, where the assembly was held, and looked out at the sea of mostly black students. These highschoolers, for the most part, either did not know who he was (many black kids did not listen to his music), or decided that this successful hippie musician did not seem to care about issues like the civil rights movement and Black Power. Some students began to heckle Hendrix, who nervously fielded a few questions. He mumbled several perplexing responses and left within five minutes, booed out the door by the kids—hardly the conquering hero. The band flew to Los Angeles that day for its next concert.

The Experience tour became a revival locomotive, with Hendrix preaching new rock gospel. Everything was increasing—crowds, money, decibels, and the madness onstage and off. Everything fed the success machine. Arena crowds topped 15,000. Everywhere the band went, a trail of shattered records for gate receipts followed. Sales of *Are You Experienced?* shot past the million mark. Critics shouted Hendrix's praises. His songs filled the airwaves. *The New York Times* asked if he was "The Black Elvis?" *Rolling Stone* gave him its "Great Balls of Fire" award. Great Britain's *Disc and Music Echo,* which had once labeled Hendrix the "Wild Man of Borneo," now called him the "World's Top Musician."

"They are the same people who first laughed," Hendrix reflected. "They sat behind their typewriters rubbing their bellies. Now they have turned 'understanding.' I don't think they understand my songs. They live in a different world."

CONSTANTLY ON THE ROAD

Hendrix was living like his vaudevillian grandmother, Nora, with the road his only home, but in circumstances exaggerated to wild extremes. By now it felt as if he had played for a million people and traveled a million miles. The life had its moments. Always shy offstage, Hendrix now found it easy to meet women. Like everybody else, they sought him out. It seemed as if he was never alone. Friends, groupies, and hangers-on kept him company. Bandmates, roadies, managers, publicists, and lawyers protected the business side, which got bigger by the day. "As far as Hendrix's popularity was concerned, it was like a snowball running down a hill," Chas Chandler later said. "I'd never seen anything like it. From September '67 to July '68 he was enormous."

The pace and the perpetual dislocation, however, were exhausting. There was a predictable routine—travel, play, travel, play—but nothing felt ordered inside that routine. Life was a relentless barrage of people, places, and appointments made by somebody else, a steady diet of airplane flights, strange hotel rooms, and erratic sleep. The constant collision of onstage highs and post-show crashes made it very desirable to smooth the rough edges, seek inspiration, or just hide away by using drugs. Drug use in the music world was far from harmless. Eric Clapton, for example, would become addicted to heroin, and Beatles manager Brian Epstein had died of an overdose. But nobody stopped to reflect on these catastrophes; people were too busy getting to the next gig, partying, living the life.

Hendrix was intimately familiar with the drug culture that was, for musicians, part of the identity and part of the scene. Like many other performers, he popped his way through the rock and roll medicine cabinet of uppers and downers—not to mention marijuana and LSD—when he needed help coping with his crushing performance schedule. (Mike Jeffery was notorious for overbooking the band; during a three-year period, it played a staggering total of 550 concerts.)

With so much daily chemical input, mood swings were ramped up, and tensions rose exponentially. One night, in the middle of a show at the Xavier University fieldhouse in Cincinnati, Ohio, Hendrix's amplifiers started picking up the signal of the nearby campus radio station. The amps went haywire. Hendrix could not keep the radio chatter from bleeding through his speakers without shutting off the amps. So he walked offstage after four songs and never came back.

In general, equipment was a chronic headache for the Experience. Hendrix played so loud and pushed his gear so hard in search of his ideal sound that scores of amplifiers just blew their tubes. The Experience literally left a trail of broken guitars and blown amps across America.

HEIGHTENED DISCORD

Meanwhile, the feud that had been simmering between Redding and Hendrix since the recording of *Axis: Bold as Love* worsened. Only three weeks after *Axis* was released, the band started recording its third album, *Electric Ladyland*. Redding had chafed at Hendrix's slow, deliberate style of sorting through songs in the studio, which forced the bassist to sit around for hours, waiting to be told what to play. Finally, after Hendrix did take after take after take on what would be the album's first single, a cover of Bob Dylan's "All Along the Watchtower," Redding got so frustrated, he walked out of the session (in fact, he appears on just 5 of the 16 tracks on *Electric Ladyland*). Out on tour, Hendrix and Redding became so estranged that they began using separate dressing rooms.

Aside from their artistic disputes, money was another issue. Despite sold-out concerts and soaring album sales, the band members were still living hand to mouth, a state of affairs Redding and Mitchell bitterly resented. Hendrix, who freely lent money to anyone who needed it, mainly concerned himself with his music and had little interest in finances. "I'm so bad when it comes to money," he once said. "I force myself to save it by not knowing when it's around and not being able to get it any time I want."

From February to April on the 1968 tour, the Experience went through Washington, California, Texas, Colorado, Illinois, Wisconsin, Michigan, Maine, Massachusetts, Rhode Island, Pennsylvania, Connecticut, Delaware, Ohio, Virginia, Washington, D.C., and Canada. Hendrix and his band traveled through a country rife with ferment and political turmoil. U.S. military involvement in Vietnam was at its peak, and protests against the war, especially on college campuses, were reaching a fever pitch. Then, on April 4, 1968, the Reverend Dr. Martin Luther King, Jr., the apostle of the civil rights movement in America, was shot and killed by a sniper in Memphis, Tennessee. That evening, Hendrix was slated to do two shows at the Civic Dome in Virginia Beach, Virginia. He completed the first show, but the second show was canceled after news of Dr. King's assassination spread.

The Jimi Hendrix Experience posed on the steps of a plane along with members of Soft Machine, the Animals, and the Alan Price Set. The groups were leaving London in January 1968 for the United States. Along with the exhausting pace of touring, a rift was developing between Jimi Hendrix and Noel Redding over creative issues and money.

At the same time, riots in black communities were erupting all over the country. The Experience's next show was at Symphony Hall in Newark, New Jersey, and the band was not sure there would be a show because of the threat of violence. The police told the band to do just one show and leave. So with shots heard in the distance and tanks patrolling the streets, the show went on—but not the usual show. *Electric Gypsy* quoted Mark Boyle, who was the lighting designer with Soft Machine, the opening act for the Experience:

> Hendrix came out to enormous applause and said, "This number is for a friend of mine," and he abandoned completely his normal set. The band played an improvisation which was absolutely hauntingly beautiful. Immediately everyone knew what this was about. This was a lament for Martin Luther King. And within minutes the whole audience was weeping.... The music had a kind of appalling beauty. Harrowing music.

That night there were none of the usual histrionics. The band played about 45 minutes of blues. Then, according to Boyle: "When [Hendrix] came to the end, there was no applause. He just put down his guitar, the whole audience was sobbing, and he just walked quietly off the stage."

IN HIS OWN WORDS...

Although Jimi Hendrix's initial success came about primarily as a result of his performances at huge music festivals and, later, stadium-sized venues, he much preferred playing in small clubs. As quoted in *Electric Gypsy*, Hendrix told a reporter from the *Chicago Daily News*:

> Right now when it comes to actual playing, I like to do really funky clubs. Nice sweaty, smoky, funky, dirty, gritty clubs 'cause you can really get to the people then. All this stuff where you stand 2,000 miles away from the people and all that—I just don't get any feeling at all. But I guess we can't do that for the rest of our lives. We'll just have to play these other scenes, too. Just so long as there are people there.

THE POLITICAL

Reporters often asked Hendrix about racism, civil rights, poverty, and the riots that ravaged black neighborhoods in Los Angeles, Detroit, and other cities after Dr. King's assassination. Hendrix felt deeply about these events, but he preferred to express himself in music rather than make political statements. "Talking isn't really my scene," he told one interviewer. "Playing is."

Hendrix, however, was soon drawn deeper and deeper into the political upheavals of the time, whether he liked it or not. Civil rights demonstrators and young people protesting the Vietnam War saw themselves as part of an uprising—peace soldiers in a revolution of consciousness. They also believed in the spiritual power of music, and they conducted their revolution to the sounds of Bob Dylan, the Jefferson Airplane, the Doors, the Grateful Dead, Neil Young, Arlo Guthrie, and Jimi Hendrix. Hendrix did not insulate himself completely from these conflicts. In June, he attended a benefit at Madison Square Garden for the Martin Luther King Memorial Fund and wrote the fund a $5,000 check to help carry on the struggle for civil rights.

After going back to England for a short rest, the Experience returned to New York in mid-April to record *Electric Ladyland* at a Manhattan studio called the Record Plant. Hendrix had strong ideas about the new album and took a firmer hand, often over the objections of Chas Chandler, who worried about the cost of studio time and questioned the soundness of Hendrix's thinking. Hendrix was aiming for a major opus, a record that combined the best aspects of the previous albums with a renewed commitment to getting every detail right. His ambition was costing Chandler and the band's sponsors a fortune in studio time. Time after time, though, Chandler's objections were overruled.

The sessions for the new album turned the Record Plant into a vast living room, with friends, strangers, and other musicians dropping by in a never-ending pilgrimage to see Hendrix, feed him drugs, jam and record with him, or just hang out. The partylike ambience drove everybody but Hendrix crazy. "There was a dreadful atmosphere in the studio," Chandler later said. "There were so many people hanging around him, he couldn't be himself. We had an argument about it and he said, 'OK, no more.' Then someone would turn up at the studio with a bag of goodies and pour some more down his throat.... Things began to deteriorate." Hendrix's determination to fulfill his own vision in *Electric Ladyland* had its price: On May 8, frustrated by Hendrix's snail's-pace recording style and feeling that his counsel was no longer wanted, Chas Chandler quit as producer and co-manager and left New York. The man who had launched Hendrix's career was gone. Mike Jeffery basically bought Chandler out, then shifted operations to New York.

Despite Hendrix's perfectionism, the album progressed track by track. He had a head full of songs—so many, it seemed, that he could not get them on tape fast enough. The band was putting together enough material for two albums. But Mitchell and Redding were increasingly discontented. Redding, in fact, "stormed out" of the recording for "Voodoo Chile (Slight Return)" and does not appear on the cut; Jack Cassady of Jefferson Airplane plays bass on the recording. A songwriter and singer in addition to playing guitar and bass, Redding was also unhappy about Hendrix's disregard of his songs. He wanted Hendrix to make room on the new album for one of *his* tunes. After some prodding, Hendrix finally agreed to include Redding's straight-ahead rocker "Little Miss Strange." But it was too little too late. Redding started to think about forming his own band.

In September, the Experience released the album's first single, "All Along the Watchtower." Hendrix had taken Dylan's spare acoustic version and transformed it into an electric tour de force with a guitar solo that is considered one of the most exquisite he ever played. When *Electric Ladyland* hit store shelves on October 5, 1968, in Great Britain and 11 days later in the United States, it was a double LP, containing 16 songs on four sides. Because of the added cost, it was not the ideal formula for a hit. Still, *Electric Ladyland* rocketed to the top of the U.S. charts. Hendrix had his first number-one record.

Like its predecessors, the album was an eclectic smash, fusing rock, funk, and blues with classical flourishes and jazz sounds. From the soaring grace of "All Along the Watchtower" to the street-corner funk of "Crosstown Traffic" to the eerie, shamanlike dirge of "Voodoo Chile (Slight Return)," Jimi Hendrix showed he had few peers in his ability to merge sounds and styles into an electrifying whole. "Yeah, that whole LP means so much, you know," he told an interviewer. "It wasn't just slopped together. Every little thing that you hear on there means something, you know. It's no game that we're playing, trying to blow the public's mind or so forth. It's part of us."

The success of the album was a spectacular end to a hectic, chaotic year. To the world outside of Hendrix's inner circle, it must have portended an even better year to come. But Chas Chandler's departure was merely the first signal of more changes to come—not the least of which was the end of the Jimi Hendrix Experience.

7

House Burning Down

Jimi Hendrix began 1969 by courting disaster on British television. *Happening for Lulu*, featuring Lulu, the Scottish singer most famous for "To Sir With Love," aired live on BBC television. On January 4, the Experience made what would be its first appearance in England in months on an episode of the show; the script called for the band to play two songs— "Voodoo Chile (Slight Return)" followed by "Hey Joe"—and then Hendrix would perform a duet with Lulu. The hostess was positively swooning over her guests, who did the first song as scheduled. Then Lulu introduced "Hey Joe," gushing that it was the song that had made the group famous in England, "and I love to hear them sing it."

Hendrix had other ideas. The Experience had gotten about a minute or two into "Hey Joe" when Hendrix, having mangled the words, abruptly stopped and announced that he was done playing that garbage and instead was going to salute Eric

Clapton and the other members of the recently disbanded group Cream. With that, the band broke into Cream's "Sunshine of Your Love." Lulu gamely smiled her way through this unscripted adventure. But the show's producer was beside himself, waving madly and trying to get Hendrix to stop. Hendrix kept right on playing—right through the end credits. Although the incident appeared impulsive, Hendrix in fact had told his girlfriend, Kathy Etchingham, before the show that he wasn't going to sing with Lulu because he would look "ridiculous."

While Hendrix was touring in America, the ever-faithful Etchingham got a new flat for them, and Hendrix finally admitted to the press that he had a girlfriend—"My girlfriend, my past girlfriend, and probably my next girlfriend; my mother and my sister and all that bit; my Yoko Ono from Chester," he called her—though that hardly stopped him from continually cheating while he was on tour. A week after telling the world about Etchingham, he would stand on stage in Stockholm and publicly invite his favorite Swedish groupie, Eva Sundqvist, to his room.

PERFORMANCES HOT AND COLD

Hendrix's hijacking of *Happening for Lulu* showed that he had developed a willful streak that could cause any performance to take a playful, sullen, or even hostile turn. For Hendrix, the pressure to keep the success machine running threatened to suck the joy and satisfaction out of what he loved most: playing music. Everybody seemed to have opinions, expectations, and instructions about what he should play and how he should act onstage. Hendrix called this "pop slavery." He kept his love of performing and his sense of humor intact by throwing curves at his audience. But when his humor failed him, frustration soured into contempt. On some nights, Hendrix would simply stand behind the microphone, muttering barely audible insults at the audience. He sometimes refused to play the crowd-pleasing hits everybody had come to hear.

What turned out to be the band's final European tour began in Sweden on January 8, and (as quoted in *Black Gold*) Noel Redding noted, "On the whole, I can't understand how anyone who saw us could have liked the group.... We were very tired and very bored, and it showed." The tour would turn out to be notable primarily for two reasons: In Sweden, Hendrix would conceive a son with his student girlfriend, Eva Sundqvist. In Germany, Hendrix would meet Monika Dannemann, the woman with whom he would ultimately spend his last hours.

Controversy over the packaging of *Electric Ladyland* was not helping Hendrix's disposition. Hendrix had given the record company very specific instructions to use photographs by Linda Eastman (later Linda Eastman McCartney) for the album, plus liner notes titled "Letter to the Room Full of Mirrors"—a reference to how he saw his life as a rock star as a distortion reflected back at him. When the double album was released in Great Britain, though, the cover sported a bevy of nude women lounging like members of a harem in some erotic fantasy. Some record stores either refused to sell the album or insisted that it be packaged in a brown-paper wrapper. Worse, Hendrix was catching flak in the press for the record company's choice of imagery. "I didn't have anything to do with that stupid LP cover they released, and I don't even want to talk about it," he snapped at an interviewer.

In February 1969, the influential magazine *Rolling Stone* named Jimi Hendrix its Performer of the Year for 1968. But the paradox of that laurel began to surface in his live appearances, which grew more erratic as the new year progressed. Hendrix—under pressure to perform, to record, to earn money, to be everybody's friend—was having trouble with the multiple demands. That strain registered onstage. He could wreck an evening for one paying crowd with sloppy, grudging guitar work and halfhearted singing, then play brilliantly the next night. Audiences never knew which Jimi Hendrix would show up, but they came to see him anyway. Hendrix hated that the most because to him that meant no one was really listening; people were just there to be there. On top of this, the entire drill was getting old quickly. As Noel Redding put it, "Four years on the road with the Experience is like ten years of life." Indeed, the day after the *Rolling Stone* pronouncement, Redding began rehearsing with his own new band—composed of several musician friends—called Fat Mattress.

"In fact, the band was never exactly over-rehearsed, and it is obvious now that the electrifying 'newness' held it all together," Chris Welch later wrote in *Hendrix: A Biography*. "As soon as the nightly routine began to pall, that's when the band began to fall apart. And the rest of Hendrix's years in England and in the States were spent searching for an alternative."

JAM SESSIONS

He found one alternative in jamming. Hendrix spent more time in 1969 playing in low-key, informal settings that placed no restrictions on the set list, the song length, or the style of music played. He would walk into New York clubs like the Scene and Café Au Go Go with a guitar and spend a few hours with other players—some famous, some unknown. He could break for a beer without hassle or fuss from patrons, many of whom were, like the musicians, seeking refuge from the gawkers, groupies, and ever-increasing hype of the big-time rock scene. Hendrix could stretch out musically in these sessions, experiment, and play what he pleased. "I get more of a dreamier thing from the audience [in clubs]," he once said. "It's more of a thing that you go off into.... You don't forget about the audience, but you forget about all the paranoia."

Musicians and spectators lucky enough to be present said these impromptu jams yielded some of the most brilliant, beautiful playing they have ever heard. Hendrix, in turn, took great solace from these free-form late-night outings with strangers and friends. In the face of mounting business and personal pressures, retreating to the simplicity of his early playing days seemed to keep him stable and sane. It reminded him why he had picked up a guitar in the first place.

At this point, rumors were flying that the Jimi Hendrix Experience was about to split. Everybody denied it. But the news of Redding's new project only fed the speculation. And there was no denying that Hendrix and Redding, especially after the recording of *Electric Ladyland*, were practically at each other's throats. "Around 1969, we were so overwhelmed by money and the glamour of being so-called pop stars, we all forgot we were people," Redding later said.

Neither Hendrix nor Mike Jeffery was willing to lose Redding—not yet, anyway. So Fat Mattress got the opening slot on the Experience's next U.S. tour, which meant Redding would be playing in two bands every night. By now Hendrix was fronting the highest-paid band in the world and leaving all the commercial details to Jeffery. Chas Chandler, now married and settled down in London, retained a small financial stake in the band and turned up at numerous shows. Hendrix asked him several times to return as manager. Chandler always said no—although he did help his old friends by taking charge of a couple of late-February concerts at the Royal Albert Hall in London, which turned out to be disastrous performances. It was as if Hendrix was playing for and by himself, and Redding and Mitchell were with a completely different band.

The Experience left for New York in mid-March for a month of studio time before heading out on what would be its final North American tour. Hendrix asked Etchingham to accompany him—a first. But when she met up with Hendrix at his New York hotel, she found that he was "trailing an enormous entourage like the colorful leader of some circus freak show." Etchingham described what Hendrix called his "friends" in *Through Gypsy Eyes:* "[The women] were obviously whores, and the men all appeared to be pimps and drug dealers, with their cool shades and little spoons hanging around their necks."

One drug-dealer friend was armed with a handgun. Finally accepting the reality of their two-and-a-half-year relationship, that "there were no long-term prospects with Jimi," Etchingham immediately fled back to England. "There was no way I was going to tame him," she recalled.

That spring and summer, the Experience rolled through a series of ever-larger venues, playing arenas and stadiums. Hendrix called the indoor shows "Electric Church" and the outdoor shows "Sky Church." The collection plate at these "churches" was fat enough to make a preacher blush: The Experience pulled down anywhere from $15,000 to $100,000 per performance, depending on ticket sales and the terms demanded by Mike Jeffery, who was in a position to ask for almost anything.

Money, though, could not stop the crumbling of the band's morale—about all they shared at this point were ever-increasing drugs, including methamphetamines, cocaine and, for Hendrix at least, heroin. Besides, money was cold comfort to Hendrix, who threw cash around like confetti and seemed to care very little about how it came or went. If anything, the money just reminded him of how trapped he felt by a career he once longed for but now longed to escape. Before leaving New York, Hendrix called his old bassist friend Billy Cox in Nashville and asked him to meet him when the Experience played in Memphis. He explained how unhappy he was with Redding and told Cox he would soon call—when the time was right. A drug arrest interfered with Hendrix's plans.

BUSTED IN CANADA

At 9:30 A.M. on May 3, Hendrix landed at the airport in Toronto, Ontario, on a flight from Detroit. There, the Royal Canadian Mounted Police were waiting, and an officer asked Hendrix to open his carry-on bag; inside were plastic bags of hash and heroin. Evidence points to the drugs having been planted—possibly by a disgruntled groupie who called the authorities—since the group members had been warned that they would likely be targeted for a search. Hendrix was arrested for possession of controlled substances and released on $10,000 bail; a preliminary hearing was set for June 19. The Mounties escorted Hendrix to the gig at Maple Leaf Gardens, where he turned in a loose, confident performance for a crowd that knew nothing about the arrest.

For all the disruption, the Experience/Fat Mattress caravan hardly missed a beat. The tour crisscrossed the United States, before heading to Seattle, where Hendrix gave a brilliant performance for a hometown crowd of 15,000 at the Seattle Coliseum. After the concert, he briefly visited with his family, as he had done on his last tour. He persuaded a star-struck high schooler to drive him around on a nostalgia tour of Seattle in the kid's beat-up Volkswagen Beetle.

After another month of touring, Hendrix returned to Toronto for his hearing. Dressed soberly in a suit for the first time since his revue days, he was told that his trial was set for December 8. He then flew to Los Angeles for a performance at the Newport Pop Festival that would earn the band $100,000 for one show. The following week the Experience would play in Denver at Mile High Stadium, where it would headline the Denver Pop Festival. It would be the band's final performance. To the complete surprise of everybody there—Noel Redding included—Hendrix ended the show with this announcement: "This is the last gig we'll ever be playing together." Another 1960s supergroup had just bitten the dust.

A NEW GROUP

Noel Redding flew to London and told interviewers he had resigned. Jimi Hendrix went to his newly rented house in upstate New York near Woodstock and started putting together a new band. Hendrix wanted a group that could reproduce onstage the rich, orchestral sound he was capable of creating in a studio. But he also wanted a connection to the music, and to the musicians, which he felt he had lost in the Experience. He called Billy Cox and told him it was time, then contacted Larry Lee, another bandmate from his long-ago Nashville days. Mitch Mitchell came back as drummer. Hendrix also signed up a couple of other percussionists, Juma Sultan and Jerry Velez. Hendrix hoped his new band would give him a new lease on his career. That August he would debut the band at the Woodstock Music and Arts Fair.

Woodstock did not go exactly as planned. The band was supposed to play Sunday evening, but torrential rain and technical problems wreaked havoc with the schedule, postponing Hendrix's appearance until 8:00 A.M. on Monday. Hendrix and the band were stuck spending the night in a freezing cottage, and they were not happy about having to play early in the morning.

Still, tens of thousands of people caught the 140-minute set, according to Cox, which featured all of Hendrix's best-known hits—including "Purple Haze," "Voodoo Chile (Slight Return)," and "Hey Joe" as an encore. Hendrix's searing rendition of "The Star-Spangled Banner" at Woodstock has gone down in modern music history as a legendary performance.

Although Hendrix spoke fondly of the people at Woodstock who stayed three days to see him, he had mixed feelings about the festival itself. Three months later, he said, "Woodstock was groovy and all that, but anybody can get on a field and put a lot of kids in there and put band after band on. I don't particularly like the idea of group after group. It all starts merging together." He also came away from Woodstock realizing that his band, Gypsy Sun and Rainbows, wasn't working. The band did some recording in New York in September and also played two more gigs, one at a summer street fair in Harlem, the other at a New York City club called Salvation. But in October Hendrix summoned the five other members to his hotel room and announced that he was disbanding the group.

Mitch Mitchell returned to England. Hendrix asked Billy Cox to stay on as bassist and brought aboard an old acquaintance,

Buddy Miles, on drums. Hendrix called this new trio Band of Gypsys. It was his third lineup in the space of four months.

Hendrix spent the following year the same way he had spent the previous three: touring and recording. He crisscrossed the United States and Europe, with few breaks. He went into studios to record whenever time allowed and filled hundreds

Woodstock Defined

By daybreak on Monday, August 18, 1969, Max Yasgur's dairy farm in Bethel, New York, near Woodstock, was a scar on the landscape. Nearly a half million festival-goers had occupied the 600 acres, experiencing three days of peace and music—plus torrential rain, love, sex, drugs, food shortages, suffocating crowds, and ankle-deep mud. Now sated and spent, the crowd slowly dispersed, leaving behind a sea of muck and enough trash to choke a small city. As Jimi Hendrix and his new band prepared to climb the stage and close the festival, Hendrix's insistence on being the final act appeared to have been an unfortunate choice.

Some 300,000 people had already migrated out. The tens of thousands of music diehards who remained wandered through the tattered landscape like war refugees—yet they did not want the experience to end. Woodstock was already legendary; no future event would ever quite duplicate its mixture of music, magic, misery, spontaneity, and history. But the legend was not yet complete, as those who had left before the finale would realize to their lasting regret.

Hendrix walked onto the stage under a streaky morning sky—white Stratocaster slung over his shoulder—looking like a cosmic hitchhiker. He surveyed those who had waited three days to hear him and smiled. Members of his new band followed him onto the stage and took their places between the steel sound towers.

Hendrix had assembled the group only a few weeks before; it did not even have a name until that morning, when Hendrix came up with Gypsy Sun and Rainbows. During the weeks leading up to Woodstock, the new band's talented players were not gelling as Hendrix had hoped. Daily practice sessions only highlighted their lack of chemistry and cohesion. "I got the feeling several times during rehearsals," Mitch Mitchell wrote in his 1990 memoir, *Jimi Hendrix: Inside the Experience*, "that Jimi realized it wasn't working and just wanted to get the gig over and start again." Now the band—incorrectly introduced as of hours of reel-to-reel tapes with songs, song fragments, and extended jams. There was an urgency to Hendrix's activity after Woodstock, as if he was racing to find or finish something before time ran out.

That fall, in a bizarre occurrence, Hendrix was kidnapped from a club by two hustlers who demanded his contract from

the Jimi Hendrix Experience—took a moment to get acquainted with the roaring crowd. Hendrix gently corrected the announcer's lapse. "Dig, we'd like to get something straight: We got tired of Experience, and every once in a while we was blowing our minds too much. So we decided to change the whole thing and call it Gypsy Sun and Rainbows. For short, it's nothing but a band of gypsies."

The six-piece group tore into "Message to Love" followed by "Hear My Train A-Comin'," during which Hendrix silenced the crowd with a breathtaking show of free-form soloing, making up phrases and musical passages as he went along. It was vintage Hendrix: sounds pouring from his instrument like inner voices screaming for release. The "Voodoo Chile" may have been aging, but he was still Jimi Hendrix, a guitar-burning font of energy, an electric shaman who played the blues as if he were possessed.

Toward the end of the set, he stepped away from his microphone and, like a lonely bugler, sounded out the first notes of "The Star-Spangled Banner." The familiar melody floated out over the torn-up field, in a baleful tone that seemed to weep under layers of amplified distortion. The space between each note felt a mile wide. Hendrix took the national anthem and turned it into a national dirge. He followed the melody faithfully, then cut away from the verses to turn his Stratocaster into a war machine. The amplifiers unleashed the deafening roar of high explosives and the rattle of gunfire. Hendrix was creating a nightmarish vision of a star-spangled flag fluttering over a nation embroiled in a bloody, unpopular war in a far-off place called Vietnam. He seemed to mock and revere the national anthem's grandiosity all at once, his electrified cry echoing in the hearts and minds of the audience.

The set did not end with "The Star-Spangled Banner," but the song became Woodstock's capstone, its defining moment. In a 1989 reminiscence, rock guitarist Vernon Reid recalled: "At that moment, he became one of the greats.... He plugged into something deep, something beyond good or bad playing. It was just 'there it is.'"

Mike Jeffery as a ransom payment. Jeffery supposedly learned that the men were holding Hendrix at his own house in upstate New York. An associate of Jeffery's drove up to the house with a pair of enforcer types, overpowered the kidnappers, and rescued Hendrix, who was unharmed. Some suspected that Jeffery was behind the abduction, wanting to make Hendrix more beholden to him. In a television interview that summer with talk-show host Dick Cavett, Hendrix told him, "The more money you make, the more you can sing the blues." Cavett also questioned Hendrix about the supposedly anti-American mockery that his unorthodox rendition of "The Star-Spangled Banner" symbolized to many Americans. Hendrix simply replied, "I thought it was beautiful."

Hendrix spent much of November in the studio, amassing dozens of hours of taped recordings with Cox and Miles, on top of the material he had recorded with Gypsy Sun and Rainbows in September. As noted in *Electric Gypsy*, "By now both Warners and Track [Hendrix's British record label] were hopping up and down for some new material—Hendrix had been promising all kinds of projects to the press, but nothing had been delivered. Fragments of songs were liberally sprinkled through hundreds of hours of tape."

Hendrix was trying to use the studio time to simultaneously record and rehearse a new band. But distractions plagued him constantly. He was feuding with Mike Jeffery and, uncharacteristically, was beginning to worry that his manager might be stealing his money. (In fact, an overextended Jeffery was trying to get promoters to send deposits to him personally rather than to the band's accountant or lawyer.) Hendrix was also locked in a legal battle with Ed Chalpin, a New York producer who had signed Hendrix to a contract in his early days and now refused to accept a buyout or relinquish his rights to Hendrix's recordings. And Track Records refused to pay Hendrix his British royalties until that lawsuit was settled. To satisfy the conditions of his disputed contract with Chalpin, Jeffery

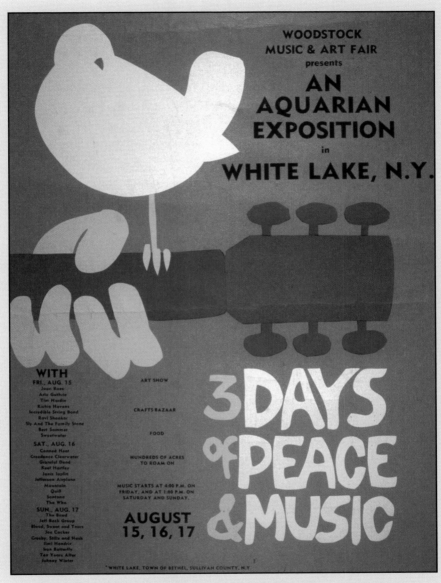

The Woodstock Music and Art Fair in 1969 was billed as "Three Days of Peace and Music." Because of weather delays, though, Jimi Hendrix and his new band, Gypsy Sun and Rainbows, did not go on till the fourth day, early on Monday morning, August 18. His version of "The Star-Spangled Banner" became a defining moment at Woodstock.

came up with an idea. Hendrix would record a live album for Chalpin with the new group, Band of Gypsys.

IN COURT

Before that could happen, though, Jimi Hendrix still had to face his drug trial. He flew to Toronto and appeared in court on the morning of December 8, 1969, dressed in a pinstriped double-breasted suit bought for the occasion. The threat of jail that had been hanging over Hendrix's head for seven long months was about to be faced. For three days, the jury heard testimony declaring that Hendrix had had no idea the drugs were inside his flight bag. The defense lawyer argued that one or more of the musician's fans, who were always pressing gifts on him, must have discreetly tucked the drugs into his bag before the trip to Toronto. The jury deliberated for eight hours, and returned with a verdict: not guilty. Smiling, Hendrix left the courtroom and flashed a peace sign at reporters waiting outside. "The best Christmas present I could have," he told them.

Three weeks later, a rhythmic beat drifted through the locked doors of the Fillmore East into the wintry wind blowing down Second Avenue in Manhattan. Inside, sound poured from the amplifiers stacked like matching skylines on either side of Miles's drum kit. Hendrix, Cox, and Miles were rehearsing full blast for the Band of Gypsys debut on New Year's Eve 1969, to a sold-out crowd. The Fillmore East's owner, Bill Graham, was the same savvy promoter who had booked Hendrix's early San Francisco shows at the original Fillmore. The Fillmore East performances—four in two days—would furnish the raw material for Hendrix's first live album, the self-titled *Band of Gypsys*.

Hendrix's gigs at the Fillmore East were uneven. The first show was so disappointing, in fact, that many in the audience walked out midway through the performance. But the second show was a complete turnaround. Quoting Bill Graham,

In this photo, Jimi Hendrix performs at the Fillmore East in the East Village of New York City. At the end of 1969, Hendrix and his latest lineup, called Band of Gypsys, played four shows over two nights at the Fillmore East. A live album of the performance came out in April 1970.

Charles R. Cross wrote in *Room Full of Mirrors*: "Aside from Otis Redding, there will never be anything like that show. The man took maybe three steps one way or the other during the whole set. He just played. And he just sang. He moved his body but it was always in time to the music. He was Fred Astaire.... There was grace but no bull." Unfortunately the tracks for the live album, which was released on Capitol Records in April 1970, did not come from that second, phenomenal show but rather from the two shows the following day. "If it had been up to me, I would never have put it out," Hendrix later said. Ed Chalpin apparently agreed, saying that—despite the brisk record sales—the album was not "up to Hendrix's normal standards." Still, *Band of Gypsys* contained several new songs and some breathtaking performances. Those two elements converged in "Machine Gun," an aggressive protest against violence in which Hendrix displayed his total mastery of technique and sound.

The new band's debut was also its peak. The trio performed just once more, a month later at the Winter Festival for Peace, an antiwar benefit with 11 other acts held at Madison Square Garden in New York. That performance was disastrous; feeling sick from drugs and unable to play, Hendrix walked offstage after two songs. End of show—end of the Gypsys. In *Black Gold,* Buddy Miles was quoted as saying that Mike Jeffery "sabotaged the Band of Gypsys because [he] wanted Mitch and Noel. He didn't want to have an all-black band, so I got iced." Billy Cox returned home to Nashville. Jeffery was immediately on the phone to Mitch Mitchell and Noel Redding, telling them the Experience was being reborn. As far as Miles is concerned, that was the beginning of the end for Hendrix.

8

Castles Made of Sand

At Mike Jeffery's urging, Mitch Mitchell and Noel Redding flew to meet Jimi Hendrix in New York. The three men met with a *Rolling Stone* reporter on February 4 to announce the Experience's regrouping and three major tours. But the "reunion" barely outlasted the interview. Hendrix had already decided he could not play with Redding, who was told to go home. The bassist, hired and fired almost in one breath, returned to London. In his place, Billy Cox agreed to join Hendrix again. The revamped Experience lineup would consist of Hendrix, Mitchell, and Cox. But Hendrix wasn't through with some earlier bandmates. On February 16, he recorded a session with Buddy Miles and Juma Sultan—much to the displeasure of Jeffery, who wanted Hendrix to focus on *his* idea of a band. Jeffery also nixed the idea of Hendrix's doing a jazz session with Miles Davis for producer Quincy Jones. Around this time, Eric Burdon of the Animals warned Hendrix that Mike Jeffery was looking out solely for his own interests. Hendrix refused to change management, believing "the devil you know is better than the devil you don't."

But Hendrix was deeply unhappy. He was tired of being a rock and roll star, tired of being "a clown." His unhappiness intensified when he learned that his old love, Kathy Etchingham, had gotten married the previous November. On March 9, Hendrix called Etchingham in London and told her he had to get out of New York; the next day he flew to London and tried to persuade her to leave her husband and come back to him. They ended up talking all night, and, Etchingham told Johnny Black in *Jimi Hendrix: The Ultimate Experience:* "He seemed slightly paranoid. He said he didn't want to prance around and be a performer, he just wanted to play music. But I know what he meant really was that he just wanted to sit down and play the blues." Etchingham turned down Hendrix's offer, but she did briefly accompany him around London while he visited some old haunts and did a few recording sessions with friends. Finally, feeling that "there was nothing left for him in London," Hendrix flew back to New York on March 19.

ON THE ROAD ONCE MORE

The 31-city Cry of Love tour featured the new Experience line-up, with Miles's band, the Buddy Miles Express, aboard as an opening act. The tour launched in April 1970 at the Los Angeles Forum to a packed house of 20,000. The fans were sticking with Hendrix, despite all the recent chaos and turnover in his career, and rewarding him with sold-out shows at arenas and festivals across the country. To cope with touring, though, Hendrix was relying even more heavily on drugs and alcohol, several times playing drunk and slurring his words. He became increasingly obsessed with mortality and told the audience at his Madison, Wisconsin, concert that "we have to get blown up, and then we go on to something better, right? Definitely. If you don't think that, you might as well die now. Oh, Lord, I'm dying."

On July 26, Hendrix returned to Seattle for a concert and reconnected the following day with his family and friends, including Freddie Mae Gautier, whose mother had taken care of Hendrix when he was just a few weeks old. Unfortunately Leon Hendrix could not be there; he was in jail for larceny. One sibling who did stop by was his 18-year-old sister Pamela, who had been put up for adoption and whom Hendrix had not seen in 17 years. Hendrix also snuck in a call to his high-school sweetheart, Betty Jean Morgan. But with nothing in common anymore, they soon ran out of things to say to each other. Hendrix left Seattle the next day for a show in Hawaii.

The Hawaii gig was not, strictly speaking, a concert. It was part of a strange counterculture movie titled *Rainbow Bridge,* whose story involved a crew of psychedelic explorers, young people who were into nature, spirituality, self-discovery, and experimental drugs. The centerpiece of this pseudodocumentary was a Jimi Hendrix concert at the base of the Haleakala volcano on Maui—a plugged-in Sermon on the Mount. The July 30 concert, called the Rainbow Bridge Vibratory Color/Sound Experiment, went well. The film was another matter. In one of the kinder appraisals, rock critic Charles Shaar Murray dubbed it "the dumbest hippie movie ever made." Although Hendrix got some much-needed rest and a break from taking heroin, which was unavailable on the island, he was extremely depressed and even talked about committing suicide. According to Charles R. Cross, when asked by the film's director, Chuck Wein, when he would next be playing Seattle, Hendrix replied, "Next time I go to Seattle, it'll be in a pine box." But his mood soon swung the other way, and when the film and his final concert in Hawaii were completed, Hendrix enjoyed an extended vacation on Maui.

Hendrix returned to New York to attend the August 26 opening of his personal recording studio, Electric Lady, on West Eighth Street in Greenwich Village. He and Eddie Kramer, the engineer, had already tried out the $1 million state-of-the-art facility. Hendrix planned to spend a lot of time there once his schedule eased. He flew to London the day after the opening.

THE FINAL CONCERTS

The Experience had an August 30 date at the outdoor Isle of Wight Festival, Hendrix's first British gig in 18 months. "It has been a long time," he told the mass audience. Despite the nostalgic mood, the concert got off to a shaky start. Hendrix was ailing with a glandular condition that had recently flared up, and he seemed distracted. The trio stumbled through its first few numbers, with Hendrix dropping lyrics, Mitchell missing beats, and Cox trying to hold everything together with his bass. Many in the audience booed. The band finally found a groove and finished strong, but the first impression stuck with the critics, who painted Isle of Wight as a failure for Hendrix.

From England, the band retraced the original Experience's path across Sweden, Denmark, and Germany. Hendrix was exhausted from the travel and still in bad physical shape. He was becoming testy before shows. In Sweden, he ran into Eva Sundqvist backstage at the concert. On October 5, 1969, she had given birth to his son, James Daniel Sundqvist, whom she

IN HIS OWN WORDS...

At the end of August 1970, Jimi Hendrix gave an interview to *Melody Maker* magazine that made it clear he was tired of playing the same old material and was looking ahead to a new musical direction:

I've turned full circle. I'm right back where I started. I've given this era of music everything, but I still sound the same. My music's the same, and I can't think of anything to add to it in its present state.... I want a big band. I don't mean three harps and fourteen violins. I mean a big band full of competent musicians that I can conduct and write for. And with the music we will paint pictures of Earth and space so that the listener can be taken somewhere.

Jimi Hendrix plays in August 1970 at the Isle of Wight Festival, in what would be his last performance in Great Britain. The band stumbled through the first few numbers before finding its groove. For many critics, though, the first impression was the lasting one, and they labeled the concert a failure.

called Little Jimi. Although she had written to Hendrix about the boy, he never replied. Now she asked him if he wanted to come home with her and meet his son, but in the crazy atmosphere backstage, he did not get the chance to reply before he was whisked away. He never got to meet the child. The concert itself was "disastrous ... really awful to watch," said Chas Chandler, who had gone to see his old band. "[Jimi] was wrecked. He'd start a song, get into the solo section, and then he wouldn't even remember what song they were playing at the time."

On September 2, the band flew to Denmark, where Hendrix was now feverish. He took a handful of sleeping pills, which left him confused and staggering around before the concert.

He did not want to perform, but eventually he was persuaded to go onstage. He stumbled through three songs before walking off, unable to continue, telling the audience, "I've been dead a long time." The audience got its money back. He predicted to writer Anne Bjørndal of Denmark's *Morgenposten* newspaper, "I'm not sure I will live to be 28 years old."

The Experience was scheduled to headline the outdoor Love and Peace Festival on September 5 on the mist-shrouded Isle of Fehmarn, in the Baltic Sea off the coast of Germany. The show was in trouble from the start, plagued by torrential rain, gale-force winds, and berserk-on-booze-and-drugs German bikers who had robbed the box office and taken over the parking concessions. Violence in the crowd delayed the band's appearance by a full day; Hendrix refused to play until calm prevailed. Organizers feared a riot. Finally the band went on around noon on September 6 and played 13 songs. It would be Jimi Hendrix's last concert.

Hendrix flew back to London—the city where he had shot to fame—and took a suite in the Cumberland Hotel near Marble Arch to rest and gather strength for the many decisions he had to make. He met up with his occasional German girlfriend, Monika Dannemann, who had tracked Hendrix down in London and had taken an apartment at the Samarkand Hotel.

HIS LAST DAYS

On September 10, Hendrix went to a party for Mike Nesmith and told the former Monkee that he wanted to start an R&B band, put together "something like Otis 'cause that's really where it's at." Nesmith told the inventor of psychedelic music that he was having a "crisis of self-confidence."

On September 11, Hendrix gave a charming, upbeat interview. "It's hard to decide what I'll do next," he said. "I'd like to have a small group and a large one, and maybe go touring with one of them." Asked about politics in music, he said, "Music is getting too heavy, almost to the state of unbearable.... When

Monika Dannemann is shown leaving the coroner's court in London on September 23, 1970. She was the last person to be with Jimi Hendrix, who died in Dannemann's apartment in the early hours of September 18, 1970.

things get too heavy, just call me helium, the lightest gas known to man." He joked about getting away from it all by living in a tent, preferably one overlooking a mountain stream.

On Tuesday, September 15, Hendrix and Dannemann went to see Eric Burdon and his new band, War, who were performing for two nights at Ronnie Scott's, a London nightclub. Hendrix wanted to jam, but he was so stoned, he was turned away. On Wednesday, Hendrix met with Chas Chandler at Chandler's apartment, telling him that he wanted to fire Mike Jeffery. "He asked me to produce for him again," Chandler recalled. "He said he was going to America to pick up some tapes for his next album. He was happy, but he had been recording for over a year and a half and hadn't really produced anything."

According to Ed Chalpin, Hendrix had asked him to fly to London to discuss his career, and they were scheduled to meet on Wednesday night, September 16, but Hendrix never came. Instead, he and Dannemann went to see Sly and the Family Stone, the reigning funk band of the day, at the Lyceum. After the show, Hendrix returned to Ronnie Scott's and finally jammed with Eric Burdon and War. It would be his final jam session.

On Thursday afternoon, September 17, Hendrix and Dannemann went shopping along King's Road, with its trendy boutiques and antiques shops. Hendrix ran into Devon Wilson, a long-standing member of his extended entourage from Los Angeles. She invited Hendrix to a party that night—to Dannemann's displeasure. Hendrix swung by his room at the Cumberland and made several phone calls, one of them to his New York lawyer, Henry Steingarten, with whom he discussed future plans; Hendrix's contract with Mike Jeffery would soon expire. He also took a call at the hotel from Mitch Mitchell, who said he and Ginger Baker, the former drummer for Cream, were going to meet Sly Stone. Mitchell invited Hendrix to join them at the Speakeasy club for a jam. The prospect excited Hendrix, who said he would be there around midnight. Mitchell waited at the Speakeasy until closing time, 4:00 A.M. Hendrix never showed.

Details about Jimi Hendrix's final hours are sketchy. According to Dannemann, she and Hendrix returned to her apartment, where Hendrix composed the lyrics to his final song—ironically titled "The Story of Life." The lyrics read in part: "The story / of life is quicker / than the wink of an eye / The story of love /

is hello and goodbye / Until we meet again." Around 1:00 A.M. she dropped him off at the dinner party that Devon Wilson had told him about earlier that day, picking him up about 3:00 A.M. But according to Angie Burdon, Eric Burdon's ex-wife, Hendrix arrived mid-evening and was determined to avoid Dannemann, saying she would not leave him alone. Whatever version is the truth, the indisputable facts are these: Sometime during the early-morning hours of September 18, Hendrix—wired from taking amphetamines earlier that night—drank some wine and then took an excessive dose of Dannemann's powerful sleeping pills. While in a deep, drugged sleep, he vomited and inhaled it back into his lungs, then suffocated.

According to Charles R. Cross in *Room Full of Mirrors*, Dannemann panicked when she awoke "and found one of the most famous rock stars in the world dead next to her.... After a few phone calls, she finally reached Eric Burdon." Burdon rushed over. After reading the lyrics of "The Story of Life" and

DID YOU KNOW?

Jimi Hendrix was initially laid to rest in Greenwood Memorial Cemetery in Renton, Washington, beneath a simple headstone engraved FOREVER IN OUR HEARTS—JAMES M. "JIMI" HENDRIX—1942–1970. However, as the years passed and the family income increased, thanks to Hendrix's posthumous record sales, Al Hendrix made plans for a grand memorial that he felt would be more fitting for his famous son. The Jimi Hendrix Memorial in Greenwood consists of three granite pillars, trimmed in rainbow marble, holding aloft a large granite dome over a life-sized bronze statue of Jimi Hendrix. On November 26, 2002—one day before what would have been his sixtieth birthday—the rock legend's body and his original gravestone were moved to the new memorial. The memorial will be the final resting place for most of the Hendrix clan, including father Al, grandmother Nora, and stepmother June. Despite strong evidence that Al wanted Lucille Hendrix to be buried in the crypt, as well, Jimi's beloved mother remains in a pauper's grave—quite by chance within sight of where her son had originally been buried.

mistakenly believing it was a suicide note, he concluded that Hendrix had killed himself. He quickly set about getting rid of all the drugs and drug paraphernalia in the room before calling an ambulance so as not to damage Hendrix's legacy. Burdon and Dannemann then left. Hendrix was alone in the room when the ambulance arrived at 11:27 A.M.

The ambulance reached St. Mary Abbots Hospital shortly after noon. An attempt was made to resuscitate him, but according to the admitting doctor, it was merely a formality. He was dead on arrival. Dr. Martin Seifert pronounced Jimi Hendrix dead at 12:45 P.M. The coroner's findings as to the cause of death: "Inhalation of vomit due to barbiturate intoxication." Jimi Hendrix was 27 years old. As he had predicted two weeks earlier, he would not live to see his twenty-eighth birthday.

Although he would have hated being buried in Seattle—a place he could not wait to leave—he had left no will. So it was his father's decision that Hendrix's body be flown home for the funeral. The pallbearers were all childhood friends, including his first manager, James Thomas. Grandmother Nora, then 86 years old, came to say good-bye with Hendrix's father, brother, stepmother, and nine-year-old stepsister. Mitch Mitchell, Noel Redding, Buddy Miles, John Hammond, blues guitarist Johnny Winter, and jazz legend Miles Davis were also among the mourners. Despite their previous differences, Redding wept during the service, and Buddy Miles was so grief-stricken that he collapsed beside the coffin. Some 200 reporters and photographers stood behind a cordon outside the church, along with a crowd of fans. A long procession then wound its way to the cemetery in the Seattle suburb of Renton. October 1, 1970, was James Marshall Hendrix's grand finale.

Stone Free

Jimi Hendrix once said, "It's funny how most people love the dead;
once you're dead, you're made for life." This was certainly true
in his case. His musical output and album sales have been
greater after his death than while he was alive. *The Cry of
Love*, Hendrix's last studio album, was released in the United
States on March 6, 1971, six months after he died. The 10-song
album, which continued Hendrix's explorations outside the
confines of hard rock, reached number two in England and
number three on the U.S. charts, where it spent 39 weeks, a
run that most living artists would envy. Scores of other Jimi
Hendrix albums were released posthumously, most of which
Hendrix would have completely disavowed.

Interest in Hendrix waned during the 1980s, but with the
advent of the compact disc, many of his recordings were
rereleased on CD in the late 1980s and early 1990s. Unfortunately,
the earliest reissues are quite poor; *Electric Ladyland* particularly

suffered, with tracks placed out of their correct order. This reflected the original LP running order, when double albums were pressed with sides 1 and 4 on one LP and sides 2 and 3 on the other so that the records could be placed on an automatic turntable and played in sequence by turning them over only once.

THE SOUND OF THE '60S

Although Hendrix's music is timeless, few artists are as closely identified with the spirit of the 1960s. "Purple Haze," "Voodoo Chile," and his astonishing version of "The Star-Spangled Banner" reappear in American culture like the sirens of a lost age. Hendrix wrote the soundtrack for a decade, and despite his fears of being passed by, his music has lasted into the generations that followed. The images of Jimi Hendrix wringing notes from his trademark Stratocaster have become almost as familiar as George Washington's face on a one-dollar bill.

Those who have criticized Hendrix's politics—or lack of politics—and his naïveté about the world have overlooked the motivating power of his music. Grounded in blues, the idiom of the poor, it was a voice of release, a "cry of love" that, like all great blues, transcended the pain and the physical hardships that gave the music its soul. Hendrix transmitted what he heard inside him back to the limitless universe he seemed to capture and channel through his playing. For some listeners, this was nothing less than revolutionary.

Hendrix was a charming, unassuming genius who explored life through his music. The restless creativity that led to overwhelming frustration in the face of his "wild man of rock" persona would eventually see him grow tired of rock's straightjacket. Which leads to the question: What kind of cosmic rock-blues-funk-jazz would he be making today? We will never know, but we can only be grateful that, for a short while, at least, such a remarkable man walked this earth.

His influence resounds in the playing of every guitarist schooled on his licks, and his leading disciples have included

Figures from Jimi Hendrix's past—(from left) Noel Redding, former girlfriend Kathy Etchingham, and the Who guitarist Pete Townshend—look out a window at the house in Mayfair, London, where Hendrix used to live. They were at the home for the 1997 unveiling of a plaque on the site by the conservation group English Heritage.

Stevie Ray Vaughan, Eddie Van Halen, Prince, Vernon Reid, Eric Johnson, Joe Satriani, Mike Stern, Pat Metheny, John Scofield, Steve Vai, and Mike McCready. Each of these musicians has paid tribute to Jimi Hendrix, either by covering his songs or quoting his style. Other musicians covering his songs have included Eric Clapton, John Lee Hooker, and funk masters George Clinton and Bootsy Collins. Hendrix created a "Seattle sound" long before the rise of such grunge bands as Nirvana, Pearl Jam, and Soundgarden. His presence in music as well as his influence on dress and theatrics is unmistakable. "I've been imitated so well, I've heard people copy my mistakes," Hendrix once said.

A MASTER OF THE GUITAR

Hendrix constantly looked for new sounds and ways to explore fully the expressive possibilities of his guitar and electronic effects. Electronics engineer Roger Mayer, with whom Hendrix had a long-standing relationship, developed several devices for him, including the Axis fuzz unit, the Octavia octave doubler, and a vibrato unit, called the UniVibe. Hendrix frequently used these devices in combination, giving his sound a distinctive blend of volume and intensity along with precise control of feedback and revolutionary guitar effects. He was also an innovator: The dominant sharp nine chord (aka Foxy Lady chord), string bending, octave playing, pull offs, and harmonics—Hendrix used virtually every part of his guitar (think old blues or even flamenco players)—feedback, reverb, scraping

A Valuable Legacy Contested

Jimi Hendrix died without making a will, leading to a number of court battles through the decades. Soon after Jimi's death, Mike Jeffery informed Al Hendrix that there was barely $20,000 due him, which—considering the millions that Jimi had earned—seems to support the allegations that Jeffery had robbed his superstar blind. But Mike Jeffery died in a plane crash off the coast of Spain on March 5, 1973, forever eluding accountability. Al then handed over financial control of his son's legacy to a lawyer named Leo Branton. Meanwhile, producer Alan Douglas, who had done some work with Jimi, was brought in to put together a number of posthumous albums using Jimi's unreleased material.

After nearly two decades of entrusting management of Jimi's estate to Branton, Al began to question the arrangement and sued Branton. A settlement was reached in 1995, and Jimi's family finally secured the rights to all the material he had left behind. Their struggle to safeguard Jimi's legacy was spurred by the remarkable freshness—and the lucrativeness—of his appeal. His albums continue to sell 3 million to 4 million copies a year, and his CDs, DVDs, and likeness generate some $8 million annually—putting Jimi Hendrix near the top of *Forbes* magazine's annual top-earning dead-celebrities list.

Al Hendrix died on April 17, 2002, prompting a new legal battle for his estate, valued at $80 million. Overwriting a 1996 will, in which Leon and Janie Hendrix received equal shares of about 25 percent each, Al's later will and scratching his pick across strings, and using the wa-wa pedal in completely new ways were all invented by Hendrix. And, of course, he was the single greatest innovator of a sound in the studio.

His influence reaches far beyond the fretboard, however. Despite his lack of musical training, Hendrix's sense of melody, composition, and song structure have filtered into the highly complex and formalized world of jazz. He blew down the fire-walls between jazz, rock, blues, and rhythm and blues. Even at the height of his rock career, he was winning the admiration of talented jazz artists who saw him moving very deliberately

bequeathed Jimi's estate in a trust to his adopted daughter; her brothers and sisters were also beneficiaries. This time around, Leon was left nothing but a single gold record of Jimi's. Leon filed suit, alleging that his stepsister "interfered with Leon's inheritance expectancy" by turning Al against him and convincing him that Leon wasn't actually his son. Leon was unable to challenge the will himself, not having the funds to hire lawyers, but he found a champion in a local real estate developer, who spent several million dollars on Leon's behalf; he also rescued Jimi's boyhood home from the wrecking ball and plans on restoring it. But despite his attorneys' efforts, the courts ruled against Leon. According to the *Seattle Post-Intelligencer*, on September 24, 2004, a King County Superior Court judge ruled that Al was of sound mind when he rewrote his will, and "Leon Hendrix didn't prove that his stepsister Janie Hendrix unlawfully coerced their late father Al into denying Leon and his children a place in the estate."

Other family members, however, had also claimed that Janie and her cousin Robert were unfit to run the trust, saying the two refused to disburse money to them while they used estate money for inflated salaries, luxury cars, and no-interest loans. The judge agreed, ruling that the pair so badly mismanaged trust funds that they would be legally removed from control of some of the trusts that Al Hendrix established. Perhaps it was not the victory Leon had desired, but it was a partial vindication. As of this writing, Leon has filed an appeal and awaits a final judgment.

Al Hendrix, Jimi Hendrix's father, is seen speaking at the funeral of Chas Chandler in July 1996 in Cullercoats, England. In 1995, Al Hendrix and his family secured the rights to all of the material Jimi had left behind.

in their direction. "Hendrix would have been one of the jazz greats," the legendary trumpeter Miles Davis once declared.

Jimi Hendrix often seemed like a tourist on his own bus, going wherever the road led, leaving details to others. It was a posture that seemed to fit his gentle, undemanding nature and his live-and-let-live outlook. Increasingly, though, Hendrix was trying to convey love, peace, harmony, and tolerance through his playing. These were concepts he clung to in confusing, hostile times, and music was his way to share those ideals. "I can't express myself easy in conversation—the words just don't come out right," he once said. "But when I get up on stage—well, that's my whole life. That's my religion."

1967 *Are You Experienced?*

Axis: Bold as Love

1968 *Electric Ladyland*

1969 *Smash Hits*

1970 *Band of Gypsys*

1971 *Monterey International Pop Festival* (remastered 1992)

The Cry of Love

Rainbow Bridge

Isle of Wight

1972 *Hendrix in the West*

War Heroes

1973 Soundtrack from the film *Jimi Hendrix*

1975 *Crash Landing*

1978 *The Essential Jimi Hendrix*

1979 *The Essential Jimi Hendrix, Vol. 2*

1980 *Nine to the Universe*

1982 *The Jimi Hendrix Concerts*

1988 *Radio One*

1989 *Jimi Plays Monterey Live*

1995 *Voodoo Soup*

2000 *The Jimi Hendrix Experience* (boxed set)

2001 *Voodoo Child: The Jimi Hendrix Collection*

2003 *Jimi Hendrix Experience: Paris 1967/San Francisco 1968*

2005 *Jimi Hendrix Experience: Live at the Isle of Fehmarn*

SELECTED DVDS

A Film About Jimi Hendrix (1973 documentary; remastered on DVD, 1999; deluxe two-disc edition, 2006)

Jimi Hendrix Band of Gypsys: Live at Fillmore East (1970; remastered on DVD, 1999)

Jimi Hendrix: Electric Ladyland (1997)

Jimi Hendrix: Live at Woodstock (1970; remastered on DVD, 1999)

Rainbow Bridge (1971; remastered on DVD, 2000)

Woodstock: 3 Days of Peace & Music (1970; Director's Cut remastered on DVD, 1997)

1942 Born Johnny Allen Hendrix on November 27 in Seattle, Washington

1946 Renamed James Marshall Hendrix by his father on September 11

1948 His brother Leon is born on January 13

1951 Al and Lucille Hendrix divorce on December 17; Jimmy and Leon begin living with their father

1958 On February 1, Lucille Hendrix dies at age 32; Jimmy is 15

1959 Receives his first electric guitar as a gift from his father; enrolls in Garfield High School; joins a local band, the Rocking Kings

1960 Drops out of high school on October 31; the Rocking Kings evolve into Thomas and the Tomcats

1961 Enlists in the U.S. Army in May and is later assigned to the 101st Airborne Division

1962 With Billy Cox, forms the King Kasuals at Fort Campbell, Kentucky, and plays at venues on and off the base; receives an "undesirable" discharge from the army

1963 Begins career as a professional guitarist, playing behind established artists like Jackie Wilson, Sam Cooke, Hank Ballard, and Little Richard; heads for New York City

1964 Wins first prize in the Amateur Night Contest at the Apollo Theater in Harlem; begins to tour with the Isley Brothers

1965 Tours with Little Richard for several months; joins Curtis Knight and the Squires

1966 Forms his own band, Jimi James and the Blue Flames; meets Chas Chandler and agrees to let Chandler be his manager; travels to London and forms the Jimi Hendrix Experience; band debuts in France in October and releases its first single, "Hey Joe," in December; Al Hendrix remarries Ayako "June" Jinka and adopts her young daughter, Janie

1967 The Jimi Hendrix Experience releases its first album, *Are You Experienced?,* and makes U.S. debut at the Monterey International Pop Festival; releases second album, *Axis: Bold as Love*

1968 The Jimi Hendrix Experience launches its first U.S. tour as a headline act and records its third studio album, *Electric Ladyland*

1969 The February issue of *Rolling Stone* names Jimi Hendrix as the Performer of the Year for 1968; in May, Hendrix is arrested at the Toronto International Airport on charges of possession of controlled substances; at the June 29 performance at the Denver Pop Festival, Hendrix announces the end of the Jimi Hendrix Experience; plays at Woodstock in August with his new group, Gypsy Sun and Rainbows; on October 5, James Daniel Sundqvist (aka Jimi Hendrix, Jr.) is born; on December 10, Hendrix is found not guilty of drug possession

1970 By the end of January, Band of Gypsys is disbanded; on February 4 it is announced that the original three members of the Experience are regrouping—but it never happens; instead, a new Experience is formed; Jimi Hendrix embarks on his last U.S. tour; releases *Band of Gypsys* album; dies on September 18 in London, England; his body is flown back for burial in Greenwood Memorial Cemetery in Renton, Washington, with a simple marker

1975 Eva Sundqvist sues to establish that Jimi Hendrix was her son's father; although the Swedish court rules in her favor, an American court rules against her, saying that a blood test could not be carried out to establish paternity

1976 Al Hendrix changes his mind and recognizes James Daniel Sundqvist as his grandson

1978 The Hendrix estate agrees to pay Eva Sundqvist about $1 million

1995 After a legal battle of nearly two decades, Al Hendrix regains the rights to Jimi's musical legacy; Experience Hendrix, the company that owns and administers the rights to Jimi Hendrix recordings, songs, and related properties, is created by Al and Janie Hendrix

2002 Al Hendrix dies at age 82 in April; his 1996 will gave his son Leon 24 percent of his estate; however, the will was rewritten in 1998 and leaves Leon just a single gold record; Leon files a lawsuit on August 16 against the Hendrix estate to reclaim what he believes is his "rightful heritage"; in November, Jimi's remains are reinterred in a new million-dollar memorial

2003 *Rolling Stone* names Jimi Hendrix as "The Greatest Guitarist of All Time" in its July 2003 issue

2004 Leon Hendrix loses his lawsuit against the Hendrix estate; Janie chooses the gold record that is due Leon, and gives him a Jimi Hendrix compilation album issued posthumously, not one that has any historical value

Black, Johnny. *Jimi Hendrix: The Ultimate Experience.* New York: Thunder's Mouth Press, 1999.

Cross, Charles R. *Room Full of Mirrors.* New York: Hyperion, 2005.

Henderson, David. *'Scuse Me While I Kiss the Sky: The Life of Jimi Hendrix.* New York: Bantam, 1981.

Hopkins, Jerry. *Hit & Run: The Jimi Hendrix Story.* New York: Perigee, 1983.

Knight, Curtis. *Jimi: An Intimate Biography of Jimi Hendrix.* New York: Star, 1974.

McDermott, John. *Jimi Hendrix Sessions: The Complete Studio Recording Sessions, 1963–1970.* Boston: Little, Brown, & Company, 1995.

Mitchell, Mitch, and John Platt. *Jimi Hendrix: Inside the Experience.* New York: St. Martin's, 1990.

Murray, Charles Shaar. *Crosstown Traffic: Jimi Hendrix and the Post-War Rock 'n' Roll Revolution.* New York: St. Martin's, 1989.

Roby, Steven. *Black Gold: The Lost Archives of Jimi Hendrix.* New York: Billboard Books, 2002.

Sampson, Victor. *Hendrix: An Illustrated Biography.* London: Proteus, 1984.

Shapiro, Harry, and Caesar Glebbeek. *Jimi Hendrix: Electric Gypsy.* New York: St. Martin's, 1992.

Welch, Chris. *Hendrix: A Biography.* New York: Flash, 1973.

WEBSITES

Early Hendrix
www.earlyhendrix.com

Hendrix and the Press
www.emplive.org/explore/hendrix_press/index.asp

"Jimi Hendrix and the Chitlin' Circuit"
www.soul-patrol.com/funk/jh_chitlin.htm

Jimi Hendrix biography
www.inet.hr/~abubalo/biogrphy/biogrphy.html

Military records on Jimi Hendrix
www.thesmokinggun.com/archive/0803051jimi1.html

The Official Jimi Hendrix Website
www.jimihendrix.com

page:

3: Pennebaker / Photofest
8: Getty Images
19: Getty Images
21: Getty Images
27: Time Life Pictures/
     Getty Images
39: Associated Press
45: Getty Images
53: Getty Images
57: Getty Images

60: Associated Press, AP
65: Getty Images
71: Getty Images
87: Getty Images
89: Reuters
95: Getty Images
97: Associated Press, AP
103: Associated Press,
     PAMPC PA
106: Associated Press

Cover: Getty Images

About the Author

Dale Evva Gelfand has been a writer and freelance editor for some 25 years. She is the author of *Charlemagne* (Ancient World Leaders series) and the coauthor of *Coretta Scott King* (Black Americans of Achievement, Legacy Edition, series), for Chelsea House Publishers. She has also written a number of books about nature and gardens—including *Grow a Hummingbird Garden*, *A Little Book of Flowers*, *Building Bat Houses*, and *Creating Habitat for Backyard Birds*. When not reading basically anything she can get her hands on, she can be found planting gardens, hiking through the woods, and photographing the natural world around her house in upstate New York.

787.87166 H498G

Gelfand, Dale Evva, 1944-
Jimi Hendrix
Montrose ADU CIRC
10/06